Longshots

THE MOST UNLIKELY
CHAMPIONSHIP TEAMS
IN BASEBALL HISTORY

THE MOST UNLIKELY CHAMPIONSHIP TEAMS IN BASEBALL HISTORY

PETER WEISS

BOB ADAMS, INC.
PUBLISHERS
Holbrook, Massachusetts

Published by Bob Adams, Inc.
260 Center Street, Holbrook, MA 02343

ISBN: 1-55850-160-6

Printed in the United States of America

J   I   H   G   F   E   D   C   B   A

Dedicated to the Bitter Four

"It ain't over till it's over."
— Yogi Berra

FOREWORD
BY ROD BEATON

We would like to believe all the upbeat homilies we hear as children.

"You can grow up to be anything you want."

"People do make a difference."

"Slow and steady wins the race."

By adolescence, however, the homilies have been discovered to be trite and hollow. Except perhaps in baseball.

Every generation has an example or two of a team that grows up to be everything it aspires to be, where a player or two makes a difference and where slow and steady wins a pennant race.

There is nothing in sports quite as captivating as a longshot champion, even a longshot that nearly wins. A team like that kind of restores your faith in the wisdom of your parents and teachers. It certainly restores your faith in baseball.

I remember working in New York City in 1969, a recent high school graduate from Delaware working as a hospital orderly to save up for a freshman year of college. The last two summers had been rocked by urban violence across the nation. But what the Amazin' Mets were doing that summer rendered an extraordinary sweetness to every Manhattan day. New York City became attractive even to an outsider who generally thought the town and its teams were repugnant (a feeling shared by more than a handful of Americans).

This was the summer in which humankind sent a man to the moon for the first time. This was the summer in which a generation sent long-haired emissaries in full flower to three days of music in upstate New York—to a little place near Woodstock.

This was also yet another summer in which helmeted emissaries of that same generation were dying in Southeast Asian swamps—a summer in which the cities and campuses were still near combustion.

But the Mets were a unifying force. From Bobby Seale and the Panthers to Richard Nixon and his henchmen, Americans had to shake their head in wonder as Tommie Agee, Bud Harrelson, and a kid with a one-of-a-kind arm named Seaver overtook yet another Chicago Cubs also-ran.

It was baseball. It was a longshot. It was what the pennant race promises every spring and delivers in an occasional, magical summer.

Peter Weiss has been thoughtful enough to poll sportswriters and compile a collection of ten of the most captivating and classic longshot teams in major league history. Weiss has already established his bonafides with *Baseball's All-Time Goats*, a book that followed a format comparable to this one.

It's a good read, just as these teams were good entertainment. They are stories that cannot be told too often. They remind us of baseball's possibilities—and that hope does in fact spring eternal.

Our teachers and parents were right, after all.

Rod Beaton
September, 1992

AUTHOR'S PREFACE

In the wake of the 1991 World Series, I started to remember that baseball could actually be inspirational.

During the previous few years, I had grown more and more cynical and disenchanted with the game (or should I say *business*?) of baseball. The Pete Rose gambling fiasco lowered a dark cloud over the game. (Even worse was the way Rose's case was dealt with.) Free agency continued to send salaries into the stratosphere and smash any remaining concept of team loyalty. Young kids began trading baseball cards based on the latest monetary "value" dictated by a glossy price guide. "What's going on here?" I thought. "What about the game itself?"

The game itself, it seemed to me, was suffering. Inspirational teams became fewer and farther between. The Oakland A's were the closest thing baseball had to a dynasty, but it was a different dynasty than the Yankees of the 1950s or even the Orioles of the early 1970s. You got the feeling that established superstars wouldn't *really* hustle unless it was their option year—or there was a big bonus in the works for them.

But 1991 changed all that—and hopefully not temporarily, either. The Braves and Twins battled it out in baseball's only "worst-to-first" World Series. Both teams had finished in the basement of their respective division in 1990. There was some truly great baseball to be seen during each team's miraculous journey to the top of the standings. The World Series itself was among the best of all time. In seven grueling games—three of which went to extra innings—the Twins overcame the Braves. Neither team, however, was a loser; these two longshots were inspirational to fans everywhere. They stepped away from all the high-gloss, commercialized aspects of the modern game and showed us that, in baseball as well as in life, nothing is truly impossible.

I was inspired.

I started poring through my baseball history books in search of the sport's great longshot teams. I called fellow sportswriters around the country and conducted an informal poll to help me select the greatest rags-to-riches performances in the game's history.

This preliminary research raised a burning question: What exactly constitutes a longshot? The answer that immediately comes to mind is a team that finishes poorly one year and makes it to the World Series the next. True enough. But that's only part of the answer. Take the 1978 Yankees, for example. In 1977, they were hands-down the best team in baseball, tearing through the playoffs and winning the World Series. But the odds were stacked heavily against them the following year, because of in-team feuding, injuries, and the emergence of the Boston Red Sox as a powerhouse club. Early in the season the Red Sox held a gigantic lead over the Yanks—a lead not even the most optimistically deluded Yankee fan could hope to see disappear. But the Yankees got a new manager, got healthy, and took advantage of the striking New York newspaper writers to whittle away at the lead. The team earned a spot in this book by rising above their problems and taking the world championship against all odds. Even though the big-money game had already started, it *was* inspiring ballplaying.

After carefully weighing the game's greatest Cinderella stories against each other and further consulting the country's best sportswriters, I was finally able to select the cream of the crop. Then, I went through hundreds of old standings and boxscores on microfilm in order to plot the teams' respective paths of success. What I found in the process were some classic stories that even the most jaded baseball junkies will want to catch up on.

Writing this book made me want to have a game of catch in the backyard. It reminded me of the game's simpler days—when it was just a game. It felt good. I hope it makes you feel the same way.

Peter Weiss

Brookline, Massachusetts

October, 1992

ACKNOWLEDGMENTS

I could not have completed this book without the help of some of the top sportswriters around the country. I sincerely thank them for taking time out of their hectic schedules and giving me a hand.

A few sportswriters went above and beyond the call of duty with this project and deserve to be singled out. Pete Cava of *International Sports Associates* went way out of his way to offer extensive insight into some of the "honorable mention" longshot teams, as well as the more mainstream ones. Bill Ballou of the *Worcester Telegram* came up with some great forgotten tidbits about the '67 Red Sox drive. John Perrotto of the *Beaver County Times*, Bill Tanton of the *Baltimore Evening Sun*, Stan Hochman of the *Philadelphia Daily News* and Jack McCaffery of the *Delaware County Daily Times* also contributed memorable anecdotes here and there.

Thanks to Dan Shaughnessy of the *Boston Globe*, who for three . years has been readily available and willing to offer valuable advice and assistance.

Rod Beaton of *USA Today* was very nice to write this book's foreword and to provide obscure anecdotes. Thanks again, Rod, for taking the time to contribute.

Several friends and relatives assisted me by giving a local perspective to some of the longshot teams. Dave Hower put me in touch with his father, Condit Hower of Darien, Connecticut; Condit reminisced over the phone about being a New York baseball fan during the wild 1951 National League pennant race. Likewise, Paul Hyde of Golden Valley, Minnesota came through with some stories and insight that only a hardcore Twins fan could provide. More-than-hardcore Yankees fan Mike Griffin filled me in on his view of the Bronx Bombers' 1978 drive. John Coyle, who relocated to Atlanta just in time for the Braves' historic pennant run, contributed some great first-hand recollections of the 1991 season. Also, Chip Ainsworth, who covered the A.L. East race in 1978 for the *Valley Advocate*, sent me some clippings of his stories concerning that gut-wrenching season.

I'd like to acknowledge the late John Warner Davenport, author of *Baseball's Pennant Races: A Graphic View*. This rare self-published volume proved invaluable in helping me visualize and gauge every pennant race between 1901 and 1980. Though I never had the opportunity to speak with Mr. Davenport, I owe him a debt of gratitude for creating a unique and immensely helpful reference book.

When it came to the process of putting the book together, publisher Bob Adams showed great faith and edit-man Brandon Toropov, as usual, pulled rabbits out of his hat to prepare the manuscript. Chris Ciaschini and Peter Gouck were simply production wizards. The publicity gang of Lisa Fisher, Shawn Barber, and Alina Stankiewicz are top-drawer and always great to work with. I'm also very grateful to my neighbor and colleague Lynne Griffin for playing the unusual role of courier with various parts of the manuscript. A thousand thanks go out to these folks and everyone else at Bob Adams, Inc.

Thanks to the respective staffs of the Boston and Brookline, Massachusetts Public Libraries for assistance with the sometimes moody microfilm viewers. Adam Reich of the *Boston Globe* sports department helped me out by providing some last-minute statistics.

Last spring, Mr. Dean Whitney earned a heap of relieved thanks when he got the nasty viruses out of my computer. Christian Winter came through in a big way when he lent me his computer in Bethesda, Maryland. Chris Harges also deserves computer-related thanks for his tireless software assistance.

Thanks to my Dad for taking Chris, Marc, and me to many Red Sox games over the years (and still going strong) and to my mother for making sandwiches for the rides. (Sometimes Mom joins us at the games, for which she has my utmost respect.) As always, Cathy and Peter Winter are wonderful people, superlative hosts, and extraordinary relatives. For as long as I can remember, my grandfather Fred Coyle has provided great historical perspective as well as good chow at the Lobster Pot in Bristol,

Rhode Island.

Most of all, I want to thank my wife, Melissa. Throughout this project, Mel was wonderfully encouraging and supportive. Thanks for being so great.

CONTENTS

CHAPTER ONE

BRAVE NEW WORLD

THE 1914 BOSTON BRAVES

THE YEAR BEFORE . . .

Final 1913 National League Standings

TEAM	W	L	PCT	GB
New York	101	51	.664	—
Philadelphia	88	63	.583	12½
Chicago	88	65	.575	13½
Pittsburgh	78	71	.523	21½
Boston	**69**	**82**	**.457**	**31½**
Brooklyn	65	84	.436	34½
Cincinnati	64	89	.418	37½
St. Louis	51	99	.340	49

*"Nobody—nobody in Titus, Alabama, any-
way—believed that anybody could beat the
Athletics that year . . . We pondered that one
for a long time."*

— HALL OF FAMER JOE SEWELL
ON THE 1914 WORLD SERIES

In a National League era dominated by the New York Giants, the hapless Braves of Boston were the anti-Giants. 1911 saw them finish 54 games behind New York. They "improved" to 52 games back the following year.

Boston baseball enthusiasts tolerated this National League performance. After all, they had a brand-spanking new facility known as Fenway Park to house their mighty American League Red Sox. In the game's early days, the Red Sox shared the stage with the Philadelphia Athletics as one of the A.L.'s ruling teams; at one point the Red Sox won four World Series in eight years. (Bear in mind that this was before Sox owner Harry Frazee ruined his franchise by selling a young southpaw phenom named Babe Ruth to the Yankees in order to finance a Broadway production of *No, No, Nanette*.) The Braves had tough competition.

Attendance at the Braves' South End Grounds on Walpole Street was nothing to brag about, but a few eyebrows perked up in 1913 when the lowly Braves dragged themselves out of the basement to finish a somewhat respectable fifth place and just a handful of games below the .500 mark.

New Braves manager George Stallings was primarily responsible for this pleasant turnaround. But those fans who did notice the Braves' marked improvement weren't interested enough to note the reasons for it. Boston fans were still preoccupied with the much more dependable crosstown Red Sox. The Sox, after all, knew how to reach the big games—and they knew how to win them.

"Gentleman George" Stallings was born in Augusta, Georgia in 1867. He graduated from the Virginia Military Institute, and attended medical school at Baltimore's College of Physicians and Surgeons. As a ballplayer with Brooklyn and Philadelphia, he appeared in only seven major league games and posted a .100 lifetime batting average.

He was a surely a scrappy and innovative manager. Not afraid to challenge baseball's rigid status quo, Stallings pioneered the platoon system by employing lefthanded and righthanded hitting combos in the field. He was scoffed at by other managers for this peculiar innovation, but Stallings held his ground and saw his ideas work. Before being hired by Boston, Stallings had turned the last-place New York Highlanders into second-place contenders. Jimmy Austin, who played his first two years under Stallings for the Highlanders in 1909 and 1910, remembered him in *The Glory of Their Times* as "A fine manager. One of the best."

Although Gentleman George was a snappy dresser—he refused to don a team uniform, and sat in the dugout wearing a three-piece suit and derby—he had a salty tongue and a hair-trigger temper. Journalist Tom Meany once wrote, "No man, not even John McGraw or Leo Durocher, ever reached the heights of invective stormed by George. He could fly into a schizophrenic rage at the drop of a pop fly."

"Talk about cussing!" recalled Austin, "Golly, he had 'em all beat . . . Once, in a game, he gave me a real going over. Later that night he called me in and said, 'Jim, I'm sorry about this afternoon. Don't pay any attention to me when I say those things. Just forget it. It's only because I get so excited and want to win so bad.'"

Stallings' yearning to win paid off as the Highlanders finished second in 1910, but that was a couple of weeks after he had quit over a dispute with first baseman Hal Chase and the team owner. Without Stallings—and, ironically, under the leadership of Mr. Chase—New York finished a distant sixth the next year.

Stallings spent the next two years out of baseball. In 1913 he was offered the unenviable job of managing the Boston Braves. He jumped on it. The good news was that under Stallings the 1913 Braves avoided the dreaded basement. It marked the first time in five years that the Braves had not finished last. The bad news was that all season long they could never once boast of a .500 record.

There were a few standouts. Rabbit Maranville, in his first full major league season, established himself as a first-class shortstop and a gutsy team leader. Maranville would go on to play 23 years in the majors for five teams and set numerous fielding records. He was elected to the Hall of Fame in 1954.

The 1913 Braves pitching staff led the majors by pitching an astounding (by today's standards) 105 complete games. In addition, they posted a collective 3.19 ERA—also impressive. All in all, it was an encouraging season. But it was nothing spectacular.

★ ★ ★

Though his Boston debut in 1913 was strong, Stallings refused to ride things out. He wanted a winner in 1914, and oversaw dramatic personnel changes within his front line in order to get one. First baseman Hap Myers left the club to play for Brooklyn in the newly formed Federal League. Third baseman Art Devlin was given his release and never appeared in the majors again. Likewise for outfielder "Silent John" Titus. Catcher Bill Rariden decided to head back to his home state of Indiana where he signed on with the Indianapolis Hoosiers of the Federal League. Others were released or traded. In all, only three everyday players from the previous year—Maranville, outfielder Joe Connolly, and outfielder Les Mann—remained on the roster. And still the Hub yawned.

One of Stallings' key steps before the 1914 season was to initiate the trade of second baseman Bill Sweeney to the Chicago Cubs for veteran standout Johnny "The Crab" Evers. It was a nice move. Sweeney went on to hit .218 for the Cubs in 1914 and retired after the season. Evers, on the other hand, batted .279 for the Braves that year and eventually wound up in the Hall of Fame.

Evans' sure hands in the field helped solidify a rapidly improving team, as did his spirit for winning. "My favorite umpire is a dead one," he once said. He'll forever be remembered as the archetypical "heads-up" player—feisty, quick, and knowledgeable.

In addition to acquiring Evers, Stallings made youngster Butch Schmidt the Braves' regular first baseman. Schmidt responded with a career year, batting .285 and stealing 14 bases. Utilityman Charlie Deal was acquired from the Tigers at the tail end of 1913 and wound up playing in 79 games in 1914. Rookie outfielder Larry Gilbert also made an impact, though he was out of organized ball within two years. Finally, Hank Gowdy—an undistinguished but solid journeyman backstop—was given the regular catching job when Bill Rariden left for the Federal League.

Even after this personnel overhaul, the Braves quickly returned to their losing ways in the early part of the 1914 season. They found themselves in last place in April and stayed there for months. The exasperated Stallings described his troops at this point as ". . .one .300 hitter, the worst outfield that ever flirted with sudden death, three pitchers, and a good working combination around second base." After all his work, Stallings was watching his worst nightmare come to life. On July 16, 1914 Boston lolled in the National League basement with a 33-43 record. For Braves fans, it was the bad old days all over again.

National League Standings: July 16, 1914

TEAM	W	L	PCT	GB
New York	44	31	.587	—
Chicago	43	37	.538	3½
St. Louis	42	39	.519	5
Cincinnati	39	40	.494	7
Philadelphia	36	38	.487	7½
Pittsburgh	34	38	.472	8½
Brooklyn	33	38	.465	9
Boston	**33**	**43**	**.434**	**11½**

There was, however, a ray or two of hope. The Brooklyn Superbas (precursors to the later Dodgers) were only two and a half games ahead of the Braves, and the fourth-place Cincinnati Reds were just a couple of games in front of the Superbas. In optimist George Stallings' mind, it was well within the realm of possibility that he could catch these teams and guide the Braves to another fifth-place finish to salvage the season. In all likelihood, he sensed as well that a fifth-place finish might reduce the possibility of his being sacked.

His starting rotation of no-names was actually doing quite a nice job. In fact, they were quickly becoming the talk of the league. Bill James, a 22-year-old righthander who had finished 6-10 in 1913, was already 8-6 in mid-July. James couldn't vary his pitching repertoire much, but he didn't really need to; his overpowering fastball was already confounding opposing hitters. He would end the year as one of the league's top pitchers, posting a 26-7 record and an incredible 1.90 ERA. (Unfortunately, James would go on to blow out his arm, and it would cost him his career.)

The thin-haired Dick Rudolph, known affectionately to his teammates as "Baldy," was another Brave righty on his way to a career season. In 1913, his rookie year, Rudolph won an encouraging 14 games. In 1914 he was already getting some press with his solid 10-9 record (quite respectable for a pitcher on a last-place team) midway through the season. Rudolph rapidly learned how to wear his opponents out with a great curveball and pinpoint accuracy. He wound up leading the league in victories with 27.

Rounding out Stallings' Big Three was George "Lefty" Tyler. He was only 6-8 in mid-July, but had suffered more than his share of tough losses. He'd end the season at 16-14 with a dandy 2.69 ERA.

On July 16th, Boston earned a 1-0 shutout over the Cincinnati Reds behind Bill James. Unbeknownst to the Braves or anyone else, it was the beginning of The Miracle.

★   ★   ★

Over the next two days, Dick Rudolph and lefty reliever Paul Strand each beat Cincinnati—on the Reds' home turf, no less—to complete a three-game sweep. The Reds had lost some key players, notably future Hall of Famer Joe Tinker, to the Federal League; they were now one of the league's weakest teams. As a result, no one thought much of the sweep at the time. But with Strand's 3-2 victory, the Braves found themselves out of the cellar for the first time all year on the morning of July 19th.

From Cincinnati they went to Pittsburgh for a five-game series against the Pirates. Like the Reds, the Pittsburgh squad was something of a lost cause. Brave pitching was nevertheless astonishing; offense was almost unnecessary against the Pirates. Tyler pitched two shutouts, with James and Rudolph contributing one apiece. When the dust settled, Boston had taken four out of five and had jumped from seventh to fourth place in less than 100 hours.

The strong St. Louis Cardinals were in third place at this point, six games ahead of the Braves. But Stallings' crew strung together nine straight victories, including a four-game sweep of the Cards. This streak saw the Braves reach the coveted .500 mark on July 31. Four days later Great Britain declared war on Imperial Germany, and the Great War was underway. The Braves hardly noticed. They were too busy winning.

During one of these games Stallings, one of baseball's most superstitious characters, outdid himself—and may have provided a psychological spark to help keep his team's winning habit alive.

Throughout his managerial career, when his team hit safely, Stallings had a curious habit of staying perfectly still—holding his exact position—until the next batter was retired. At one point during the Braves' midsummer ascent, he happened to be picking up a piece of debris in the dugout when a Brave reached base. Accordingly, Stallings remained stooped. The next batter got a hit and Stallings was denied the chance to stand upright. Still another batter hit safely—and the 46-year-old manager had to hold his position. Straining and perspiring, Stallings witnessed a total of ten Braves reach base before he could stand up. When he did, two players had to carry their cramp-ridden skipper back to the clubhouse. Stallings was sore for days, but the Braves had won.

With efforts like that, Boston fans finally took notice. In fact, the entire baseball world was suddenly paying attention to the Braves. Attendance at the South End Grounds shot up. The struggling cross-town Red Sox saw a slight dip in their attendance. Progressively larger headlines appeared on front pages across the country: "BRAVES IN PENNANT SCRAMBLE!" "RUDOLPH, JAMES, AND TYLER TOO!" "BRAVES WIN AGAIN!"

On August 10th, Bill James again defeated the lowly Reds, 3-1, in Boston. With that win, the Braves went from fourth place to a virtual tie for second with the Cardinals and the Cubs. (Actually, the Braves were percentage points *ahead* of St. Louis and Chicago—and were about to pad that lead.)

Boston met the first-place Giants for a three-game series at New York's Polo Grounds. The Braves' unbelievable run of 18 wins in their last 22 games had brought them from the cellar to just $5\frac{1}{2}$ games behind the Giants. This "showdown" would be the test to see if the Braves were for real. New York had been comfortably perched atop the National League for almost three months; most baseball realists believed this series would put an end to the absurd Boston charade.

It did anything but.

Rudolph shut down John McGraw's legendary Giants in the opener, 5-3. Bill James limited New York to just three runs while the Braves pounded future Hall of Famer Rube Marquard's every offering for a 7-3 victory the next day. And New York's Jeff Tesreau, who would go on to win 26 games that year, took the tough loss in the third game as Tyler shined for a 2-0 shutout. The sweep was complete; it brought the Braves within $2\frac{1}{2}$ games of first place.

National League Standings: August 16, 1914

TEAM	W	L	PCT	GB
New York	58	44	.569	—
Boston	**55**	**46**	**.545**	**2½**
St. Louis	57	52	.523	4½
Chicago	54	51	.514	5½

The broom job sent McGraw and his Giants into a tailspin. They lost nine out of ten games. On August 23rd, the Braves completed another leg of their odyssey by pulling into a first-place tie with baseball's dominant team. "BRAVES, GIANTS TIED FOR FIRST!!" read the headlines.

National League Standings: August 23, 1914

TEAM	W	L	PCT	GB
Boston	**59**	**48**	**.551**	**—**
New York	59	48	.551	—
St. Louis	62	53	.539	1
Chicago	60	53	.531	2

Over the following two weeks, New York and Boston flip-flopped as National League front-runners four times. Then came another showdown, this time in Boston. By now the Braves were commanding so much attention and drawing so many fans that they "borrowed" the Red Sox' state-of-the-art Fenway Park for home games when the Sox were out of town.

On Monday, September 7, with both teams again tied for first, 70,000 fans watched them split a doubleheader at Fenway. Rudolph prevailed in the Braves' 5-4 morning win, but Tyler lost his touch in the afternoon game. At one point Tyler nearly started a riot when he hit New York's star center fielder Fred Snodgrass with a pitch. The bruised batter trotted to first and directed a vulgar gesture toward the pitcher. Tyler responded by inciting the crowd, mocking Snodgrass with a crude re-enactment of the outfielder's well-known World Series-losing error from two years earlier against the local Red Sox. Boston fans ate it up and jeered Snodgrass. When he returned to the outfield, they howled and threw beer bottles at him.

The Mayor of Boston ran onto the playing field and appealed to the umpires to remove Snodgrass from the contest for his own safety; the request was denied. The fans finally calmed down and the Giants proceeded to pound the Braves, 10-1—to bring the two teams into a first-place tie for what seemed like the hundredth time in three weeks.

National League Standings: September 8, 1914

TEAM	W	L	PCT	GB
Boston	**68**	**53**	**.562**	—
New York	68	53	.562	—
Chicago	68	59	.535	3
St. Louis	67	62	.519	5

James beat the struggling Marquard again—the usually dependable lefthander was mired in horrific slump—this time by a score of 8-3. The Braves were all alone at the top.

George "Iron" Davis was a young righthander the Braves had picked up the previous year when he was dropped from the Yankees. Davis was a dependable spot starter who went about his business and usually got the job done. With the Braves in first, he hurled a brilliant 7-0 no-hitter against the Philadelphia Phillies in Boston. There was something in the air.

★　★　★

In the wake of Davis' no-hitter, the Braves went on yet another tear. In their next 25 games, they won 20, lost two and played three ties.

On September 30th, the Braves and Giants began a six-game series at New York's Polo Grounds that proved to be John McGraw's curtain call. Behind Rudolph, the Braves trounced the Giants 7-1 in the first game of a doubleheader. One more Brave win would clinch it, but they had to wait until the next day as the second game was a 7-7 tie, called on account of darkness. On October 1st, Iron Davis came through once again, pitching the Braves over the Giants, 7-6, to clinch the pennant.

Baseball fans around the country were dumbstruck. The Braves had crossed the final hurdle of the most amazing second half a major league team would ever have. All told, Stalling's boys won 61 of their final 77 regular season games, a .792 clip. They were hoping to add a few more victories against the Philadelphia Athletics in the World Series.

Stallings rested Rudolph, James, and Tyler for the Series, but even without that final week their numbers were awesome. From July 15 to the end of the season James went 18-1, Rudolph 17-1, and Tyler 10-6. And all this in an era when "real" starters pitched nine innings, game after game. The miracle must have been exhausting; the "Big Three" guns no doubt savored their week of rest.

Final 1914 National League Standings

TEAM	W	L	PCT	GB
Boston	94	59	.614	—
New York	84	70	.545	10½
St. Louis	81	72	529	13
Chicago	78	76	.506	16½
Brooklyn	75	79	.487	19½
Philadelphia	74	80	.481	20½
Pittsburgh	69	85	.448	25½
Cincinnati	60	94	.390	34½

★　★　★

Connie Mack's Athletics had won four of the last five American League flags and were the closest thing the young game of baseball had to a dynasty. The A's roster boasted such familiar names as Eddie Collins, Frank "Home Run" Baker, Eddie Plank, and Chief Bender. As amazing as the Braves' climb to the top had been, there were few who believed they had much of a chance against the established A's.

The Series opened in Philadelphia. Rudolph faced Bender, a future Hall of Famer who had gone 17-3 with a 2.26 ERA during the season. Apparently the pre-Series rest did well by Rudolph. He took just under two hours to pitch a magnificent 5-hitter, beating the A's 7-1. The one run (unearned) crossed the plate in the second, the result of a Herbie Moran error in right field. Moran's gaffe stood as the only Brave blemish on an otherwise exemplary day of ballplaying.

Boston catcher Hank Gowdy, a fine defensive receiver but a mediocre .243 hitter in the regular season, stunned the Philadelphia crowd in Game One by nearly hitting for the cycle. He collected a single, a double, a triple, as well as a base on balls and a stolen base. He also scored twice and knocked a run in.

Mack's crew, humiliated by Boston's trouncing in Game One, were out for blood in the second contest. But their bats could do nothing against the fireballing Bill James, who struck out eight and held the A's to just two hits. The Braves, however, were having their own trouble with Philadelphia hurler Eddie Plank. They scattered hits here and there but failed to push across a run in the scoreless contest until the ninth inning, when A's outfielder Amos Strunk lost a long fly in the sun to give Brave utilityman Charlie Deal a double. Deal, who was called upon when regular third baseman Red Smith broke his ankle in late September, stole third and scored a few minutes later on a clutch Les Mann single. One run was all Boston needed. In the bottom of the ninth, James walked a pair but struck out Schang and got Eddie Murphy to hit into a double play—Maranville to Schmidt—to end the nail-biter. The Braves were heading back to Boston with a two-games-to-none advantage over the vaunted Philadelphia A's.

After a travel day, both teams squared off at the borrowed Fenway Park on October 12 for Game Three. Lefty Tyler faced "Bullet Joe" Bush, a young righthander who had gone 16-12 for the A's during the regular season. Both pitchers fared well, giving up two runs apiece through nine innings.

In the top of the tenth, Tyler allowed the A's to load the bases for Frank Baker with two outs. Baker hit a scorching grounder off Evers' shin for a freak single that scored two runs—and seemed to put the game in the bag for Philadelphia.

But the Braves weren't through yet. The red-hot Gowdy led off the bottom of the tenth with a towering home run over the head of center fielder Jimmy Walsh to bring Boston within one. After pinch hitter Josh Devore struck out swinging, Herbie Moran walked and Evers sent him to third with a single. Joe Connolly executed a perfect sacrifice fly to bring home the tying run.

Bill James relieved Tyler; both teams went quietly until the bottom of the twelfth. The game was still tied at four when Hank Gowdy, the man who had salvaged his team in the tenth, continued at a torrid pace by slashing his second double of the day. An intentional walk, a bunt, and a wild throw to third by Bush sealed the game for Boston. Fenway Park erupted; the Braves needed just one more victory for a miracle-crowning sweep.

The next day would be remembered in Boston for decades. The Braves had charmed a nation for several months; their extra-inning-come-from-behind win in Game Three seemed to have taken any remaining wind out of the Athletics' sails. Rudolph baffled A's batters in Game Four with his mysterious curve. He allowed only one run, striking out seven. His teammates provided three runs. When Stuffy McInnis grounded weakly to Charlie Deal at third with two out in the top of the ninth, it was over. The Braves were the champions of the world.

Stallings had used just three pitchers to sweep the powerful Philadelphia squad. Together, they allowed only 22 hits in four games and racked up an astounding 1.15 ERA. Brave batters were led by Gowdy, who hit .545 in the Series and hit the only home run.

There had never been a season like it. There may never be one like it again.

For a few years the "dead-Brave" era of the early 1900's seemed to be over for good—Stallings steered them to second- and third-place finishes in 1915 and 1916—but the bottom fell out in 1917 and Boston's National League franchise did not contend again until after World War II. Shortly thereafter, of course, it was time to pack for Milwaukee and leave Hub fans with their star-crossed Red Sox.

But on October 13, 1914, baseball fans and non-fans across the country could rejoice, because God loved the game and they could prove it. The Boston Braves had gone from last place to first in 37 days and had *swept* the heavily-favored Athletics in the October Classic. The Braves endeared themselves to a young country on the verge of war and became symbolic of America's hopes, dreams, and struggles. They had set baseball's longshot standard.

CHAPTER TWO

WAR HEROES

THE 1944 ST. LOUIS BROWNS

THE YEAR BEFORE . . .

Final 1943 American League Standings

TEAM	W	L	PCT	GB
New York	98	56	.636	—
Washington	84	69	.549	13½
Cleveland	82	71	.536	15½
Chicago	82	72	.532	16
Detroit	78	76	.506	20
St. Louis	**72**	**80**	**.474**	**25**
Boston	68	84	.447	29
Philadelphia	49	105	.318	49

"I have repeatedly stated on behalf of everybody connected with professional baseball that we ask no preferential treatment—that we would be disgraced if we got it and that we desire that all laws and regulations having to do with the war shall operate upon our personnel precisely as upon the other 130 million of our population."

— **JUDGE KENESAW MOUNTAIN LANDIS (COMMISSIONER OF BASEBALL DURING WORLD WAR II)**

It wasn't easy being a baseball fan between 1942 and 1945.

Of course, scores of World War I-era ballplayers had been summoned away from the game for military duty when baseball was declared "nonessential" to the war effort in 1918. That season had been shortened by a full month, but no one thought much of it at the time. The young sport seemed pretty frivolous compared to the momentous world events of the day. But when the Second World War reared its head, baseball—as well as the whole nation—was turned upside down. This time the draft claimed *hundreds* of top major leaguers from a game that was now—unlike in the late teens—firmly established as "America's pastime."

Instead of shortening the baseball season, however, President Franklin D. Roosevelt looked to it for help. He felt that baseball should continue to help keep up America's morale during this tumultuous period. On January 15, 1942, the president wrote a letter of encouragement to baseball commissioner Judge Kenesaw Mountain Landis. The letter read in part, "I honestly feel that it would be best for the country to keep baseball going. There will [now] be fewer people unemployed and everybody will work longer hours and harder than ever before . . . And that means that they ought to have a chance for recreation and for taking their minds off their work even more than before . . . These players are a definite recreational asset to at least 20 million of their fellow citizens—and that in my judgment is thoroughly worthwhile."

So the show went on. There were a few new wrinkles, however. Mid-game power blackouts, for instance, became commonplace during night games—and they occasionally affected the outcome of the contests. In their excellent book *Baseball Anecdotes*, authors Steve Wulf and Daniel Okrent tell of an important 1942 Dodger-Giant game at the Polo Grounds that was ended by a blackout. The Giants were leading; since the Dodgers had been winning at the end of the last complete inning, however, the victory was awarded to them. Naturally, the New York crowd was furious. The fans were on the verge of rioting when a solitary spotlight cut through the darkness and illuminated the American flag. Old Glory glowed proudly and entranced the crowd. Within moments fans fell into a solemn hush and began to leave the ballpark in silence.

There were other problems. Radio broadcasts occasionally took on a surrealistic character during the war: because enemies might pick up broadcast signals, the topic of weather could not be even hinted at on the airwaves. Play-by-play announcers had to improvise witty banter during rain delays and could not tell listeners why the game had stopped. Perhaps this tactic foiled some enemy bombers; it certainly confused the listening fans.

As expected, nearly all of the game's healthy stars disappeared, one by one, to help Uncle Sam's war effort. For the most part, these players were replaced by washed-up, near-sighted, flat-footed, overweight has-beens (and shouldn't-have-beens). The major leagues may have gotten the green light from FDR, but they were without the best major league talent.

Many players were old enough to be grandfathers. On the other end of the age spectrum, there were some players who were barely out of high school; the Cincinnati Reds were so desperate for pitching that they let a 15-year-old high school kid named Joe Nuxhall pitch two-thirds of an inning in 1944. (The terrified Nuxhall gave up two hits, walked five, and didn't appear in the majors again until 1952.)

Two special cases—each tinged with front-office exploitation—marked the extreme of baseball's wartime manpower dilemma. An outfielder for the 1945 St. Louis Browns named Pete Gray had only one arm; he still managed to bat .218. That same year Bert Shepard pitched five innings for the Washington Senators, giving up one walk, three hits, and one run. Shepard had lost his leg in the war; he used a prosthesis.

By early 1944, fully 350 of the 400 established major leaguers left the playing fields for the battlefields. The newly-formed professional All

American Girls Baseball League signaled a new atmosphere for America's national pastime. Virtually nothing was the same about baseball anymore . . . except, of course, the ability of the St. Louis Browns to finish out of the money. Or so people thought.

★　★　★

Since the dawn of time, it seemed, the Browns had been 40, 50, or 60 games out of first place. The team had finished above .500 only a handful of times and had never, ever contended in a pennant race. Even before the war, the Browns consisted mostly of pseudo-players. For two generations, one could insert the words "St. Louis Browns" into just about any joke format and elicit a laugh.

Since 1920, the Browns had rented out their home field, Sportsman's Park, to the National League Cardinals. Each season, the schedule was arranged so that while one team was at the ballpark, the other was on the road. This worked out well, despite the fact that the Cardinals' attendance—they were one of the National League's powerhouses—always dwarfed that of the Browns. The Browns were such a chore to watch that in 1935 the crowds averaged just over 1,000 fans (or, perhaps more accurately, spectators) per game.

They lost and lost. The franchise always teetered on the brink of bankruptcy. People laughed at their uniforms.

During the 1940s, the lettering on the front of the white St. Louis jerseys was intersected by a thick Taco Bell-like brown and orange stripe. The huge stripe made the team name difficult to read; the home jersey said "BRO　WNS" while the road jersey said "ST.L　OUIS." This was the majors? The team was the only franchise without *any* insignia on their caps—just a few brown and orange stripes on white to go with a brown visor. Given the illegible team name and the anonymous cap, the casual (or colorblind) baseball fan often had difficulty identifying the Browns by looking at their uniforms. This may have been intentional.

★　★　★

In 1944, the St. Louis franchise packed 25 players, 13 of them *regulars* who hadn't passed the draft's physical, into its ugly uniforms. For some strange reason, they started winning baseball games.

The Browns' ragtag gang of pitchers led the overachievers' parade. Nelson Potter, who racked up a merely average lifetime .487 winning percentage in twelve big league seasons, was able to put together a career year for the Brownies in '44. The 33-year-old righthander failed the draft's physical because of a nagging knee injury, but would end the season at 19-7 with a 2.83 ERA.

New Orleans native Jack Kramer was the number-two starter. A big righthander with a better-than-average fastball, Kramer was steady and reliable in '44. He would wind up at 17-13 with an ERA of 2.49. Oklahoma-born Bob Muncrief (13-8, 3.08) and an obscure minor-league journeyman named Sig Jakucki (13-9, 3.55) rounded out the starting rotation, while George Caster held the bullpen together. According to the Baseball Encyclopedia, Caster complimented his fine 2.44 ERA by leading the A.L. with 12 "retroactive" saves in 1944; he passed away in 1955, however, five years before the term "save" was first coined.

Vern Stephens, Mike Kreevich, Milt Byrnes, and Al Zarilla led a decent offense. While none of these players would boast Hall of Fame career stats, they each posted a solid season. Collectively, they carried the unlikely Browns offense into the thick of things in 1944.

Stephens was a slick-fielding, hard-hitting shortstop. 1944 was just his third full year in the majors, but he was already an established hitter; he batted .293 that year with 20 round trippers. His 109 RBIs were good enough to lead the league. It is often forgotten that, until the emergence of Ernie Banks in the 1950's, Stephens was baseball's top slugging shortstop. He wound up playing 15 years in the majors, retiring in 1955 with 247 home runs and a solid .286 lifetime average.

Many trivia buffs remember Mike Kreevich as one of only a handful of ballplayers to ground into four double plays in one game. He was, perhaps, a natural for the Browns. "Iron Mike" was 36 years old and in the twilight of his career in 1944. Nonetheless, the well-traveled outfielder batted .301 for St. Louis that year and provided a measure of maturity for the Brownies.

Bronchial asthma kept Milt Byrnes out of the military, but in 1944, just his second major league season, he played well enough to hold down the Browns' center field position and bat .295 in 128 games. Similarly, outfielder Al Zarilla hit .299 in 44, also his second year in the majors. Although Zarilla went on to greater success after the war with the Red Sox and White Sox, Byrnes was never heard from again after the 1945 season.

Luke Sewell, kid brother of the legendary Hall of Famer Joe Sewell, had been the Browns' manager since June of 1941. In Sewell's first season as St. Louis skipper, his boys finished 31 games off the pace, tied for sixth place. There was nothing unusual about this performance; it was what Browns fans had almost come to expect.

But in 1942, when quality ballplayers began disappearing at an alarming rate, the young skipper guided his gang to a surprise third-place finish. The Browns went 82-69 for a .543 winning percentage, landing *only* 19½ games behind the pennant-winning Yankees. Not since a few weeks before the stock market crash of 1929 had the Browns finished a season with a winning record, and it had been 14 years since they had finished as high as third place. Certainly a war is not a pleasant thing. But with World War II showing no signs of stopping, the Browns found themselves poised to regain (or, more accurately) *attain* some respect in the American League. If they were going to make a run for the pennant, now was the time.

It didn't happen the next year. 1943 saw the Browns nosedive back to their usual lackluster finish. A September spurt narrowly saved them from seventh place, but it wasn't enough to get them within shouting distance of the .500 mark. They finished with a 72-80 record, 25 games behind the Yankees. Luke Sewell might have been nervous if this had been any other team. But St. Louis yawned. His job, strangely enough, was safe. No one called for a shakeup; with the Cardinals dominating the National League for the past couple of decades, local fans barely knew the Browns existed.

Not even World War II could bolster the sagging franchise . . . or at least that's how it seemed at the end of the '43 season.

After an uneventful 1944 spring training, the Browns caught some press when they set an American League record by winning their first nine games of the season. They surrendered first place to the Yankees for a brief time in late May and early June, but started to look suspiciously like an honest-to-God contending team from that point onward.

During a July 20th game against the Yankees, with his team nestled in first place, Browns pitcher Nels Potter won himself a spot in the trivia books. It seems the pitcher habitually dampened his fingers whenever he reached for the resin bag; on this particular evening, umpire Cal Hubbard took a disliking to Potter's ritual. He told Potter not to do it again, and when the pitcher ignored the warning, Hubbard threw him out of the game for throwing a spitball. Potter was subsequently suspended for ten days and became the only pitcher ever suspended for tossing a spitter. To this day, though, Potter denies any wrongdoing on his part.

Despite such setbacks, the wins were coming easily. St. Louis pitchers were breezing through complete games left and right. By early August the Brownies were perched atop the A.L. standings, enjoying their biggest lead of the season.

American League Standings: August 8, 1944

TEAM	W	L	PCT	GB
St. Louis	**62**	**42**	**.596**	—
Boston	55	48	.534	6½
New York	53	48	.525	7½
Detroit	52	50	.510	9

Then the race got tight. In late August, St. Louis started dropping easy games while the Yanks reemerged, winning nine of ten. The Detroit Tigers and Boston Red Sox were also closing in. With a month left to play, there were four contending teams within two and a half games of one another. It was anyone's flag.

American League Standings: September 4, 1944

TEAM	W	L	PCT	GB
St. Louis	**72**	**58**	**.554**	—
New York	72	59	.550	½
Detroit	69	59	.539	2
Boston	70	61	.534	2½

Sewell griped of a lazy, unmotivated team. In fairness, it should be noted that the Browns were weathering some serious battle fatigue and were certainly unaccustomed to being in the race this late in the season. It's also safe to say that 154 games was a lot to ask of some of these players. Whatever the reason, the long-awaited pennant seemed to be slipping from the Browns' grasp.

New York took advantage of a week-and-a-half of mediocre St. Louis play to regain first place.

American League Standings: September 15, 1944

TEAM	W	L	PCT	GB
New York	76	61	.555	—
Detroit	75	61	.551	½
St. Louis	**75**	**62**	**.547**	**1**
Boston	73	64	.533	3

While riding a four-game losing streak, however, the Browns caught a draft-related break. The Red Sox lost their best hurler, Tex Hughson, to the draft, as well as their remaining top-line batsmen, Bobby Doerr and Hal Wagner. The Sox, just a few games out of first when these players were called away, went on a mammoth losing streak and were never heard from again in 1944. They ended the year by going 4-14 and wound up twelve games out of first place with a flat 77-77 record. (With the devastating losses of Hughson, Doerr, Wagner, Dom DiMaggio, Johnny Pesky and, most devastating of all, Ted Williams, the Boston squad seemed to suffer the worst of all major league franchises during wartime.) The season ground on. What was left of the American League's contending teams struggled toward the pennant.

Soon after the Red Sox had called it a season, the Yankees followed suit. On September 16 and 17, the Bronx Bombers were swept in a three-game series by the lowly Philadelphia Athletics. When they followed the sweep by losing two of three to the surging Tigers, the Yanks were effectively out of the race.

Meanwhile, the Browns picked themselves up and chased the now-first-place Tigers down the stretch. For the next two weeks Detroit was able to stay one game up on St. Louis, slipping occasionally to allow a first-place tie, but never surrendering the top of the standings outright.

On the last weekend of September, the Tigers, one game up on the Browns, squared off against the Washington Senators in Detroit for the final series of the regular season. Meanwhile, the Browns were hosting the deflated Yankees for their final four games.

★ ★ ★

How inconsequential was the American League franchise in St. Louis? Although these last four games were the culmination of a stirring pennant race, St. Louis was *still* yawning. The Cardinals had wrapped up the National League pennant two weeks earlier, so St. Louis fans—like their favorite team—were resting up for the World Series. A paltry 6,172 spectators attended the Friday doubleheader at Sportsman's Park between the Yanks and Browns. The Browns, accustomed to such neglect, forged ahead, besting New York in both games, 4-1 and 1-0. The Yanks were mathematically eliminated from the pennant race.

That same day in Detroit, the Tigers had to settle for a split in their double-header against the Senators. They won the day game 5-2, but blew the nightcap 9-2. This put the Browns and Tigers in yet another first-place tie with two games remaining on the calendar.

American League Standings: September 30, 1944

TEAM	W	L	PCT	GB
Detroit	87	65	.572	—
St. Louis	**87**	**65**	**.572**	—
New York	83	69	.546	4

Then came the final two. Journeyman Denny Galehouse took the mound for the Browns in front of a more respectable if not yet unembarrassing crowd of 12,982. Galehouse had just recently become a "regular" pitcher after spending most of the season playing baseball on the weekends and toiling in a defense plant in Akron, Ohio on the weekdays. He was in peak form against the Yankees, tossing a 2-0 shutout and carrying the Browns to the brink of their first pennant. Detroit had also won that day, however, so the Browns were still tied for first going into the season's final game.

Sewell chose Sig Jakucki to start the big game the next day. More than a few Browns insiders groaned at the choice because Jakucki was a big drinker. His drinking itself wasn't really the problem; it was the timing of his drinking. All year, Jakucki had grown notorious not for tying one on after he pitched—as was the custom—but for getting drunk *the night before* his turn in the rotation. Since he was 12-9 at this point, no one had complained. But this was the biggest game in the history of the franchise, and his teammates were nervous.

That night the team trainer saw Jakucki entering the hotel with several bottles of whiskey. He stopped the pitcher and pleaded with him not to drink until after the pennant was decided. Jakucki promised not to drink that night.

The next day Sportsman's Park was filled to capacity—the first time ever for a Browns game. Jakucki looked green. It was obvious that the pitcher had had a tough night; the trainer reprimanded him and reminded him of their pact the night before. Jakucki grinned and explained that although he had promised not to drink that *night*, he had made no promises concerning the wee hours of the *morning*.

In any case, a hung-over Jakucki scraped himself off the bench and took the mound. The Yankees touched him for two runs early on, but by the end of the third inning the 34-year-old pitcher had settled down.

Around this time the scoreboard announced that the Senators had just beaten the Tigers, 4-1, guaranteeing the Browns at least a tie for the pennant. The last thing Sewell and his crew wanted to ponder was the prospect of a playoff against Detroit. They had journeyed much too far to deal with that.

The crowd, growing excited about the prospect of an all-St. Louis World Series, let out a stream of cheers. Browns outfielder Chet Laabs responded by smashing a two-run homer in the fourth to tie it up. He then added a second two-run blast the next inning to give St. Louis a 4-2 lead. Vern Stephens added a solo homer in the eighth to cap a 5-2 victory.

There would be no playoff with Detroit. The Browns were going to the World Series.

Final 1944 American League Standings

TEAM	W	L	PCT	GB
St. Louis	89	65	.578	—
Detroit	88	66	.571	1
New York	83	71	.539	6
Boston	77	77	.500	12
Philadelphia	72	82	.468	17
Cleveland	72	82	.468	17
Chicago	71	83	.461	18
Washington	64	90	.416	25

A "Subway Series" is, by definition, a World Series played between two clubs from the same city. In 1906, the Chicago White Sox beat the cross-town Cubs in the first such World Series. After that, New York City teams tangled with each other several times. Interestingly, although there were plenty of cities in the first half of the century with more than one major league franchise, Chicago and New York were the only towns lucky enough to host a Subway Series—until the Browns won the pennant, that is. In October of 1944, the Browns had the unique distinction of being in a Subway Series that—while technically possible—virtually no one believed would ever occur.

Even with the war robbing major league baseball of its top performers, the St. Louis Cardinals still had a great year in 1944. They won 105 and lost only 49 under steady manager Billy Southworth. Stan Musial—who would miss the entire next year while serving in the Navy—hit .347 in just his third full major league season, while rock-solid shortstop Marty Marion was named the National League MVP. The Cardinals' pitching staff was tops in the majors: lefty smoke-thrower Max Lanier notched a career-high 17 victories to support ace Mort Cooper (22-7, 2.46 ERA) and Ted Wilks (17-4, 2.64 ERA). The staff ERA was a microscopic 2.67.

With the Cards' experience, depth, and sheer domination of the diamond, it was difficult for even the most romantically-inclined baseball fan to believe the Browns had much of a chance against them. Nevertheless, they gave the Cardinals a run for their money.

On October 4th, Denny Galehouse—the Browns' late-September hero—pitched a great Game One. Though he gave up seven hits and four walks, he got out of jam after jam and allowed only a single run in the bottom of the ninth. Cardinal hurler Mort Cooper wasn't so lucky. He only allowed two hits in seven innings, but unfortunately for him the two hits were a successive single and homer. The underdog Browns squeaked by, 2-1.

Errors haunted the Browns for the rest of the Series. In Game Two, the Cards scored two unearned runs on four Brown errors and evened the Series up with a 3-2 victory. The Browns committed two more errors the next day but were able to push across enough runs to win the game, 6-2, and go up in the Series, two games to one. The sorriest franchise in baseball seemed poised to pull off the upset of the century.

But there would be no storybook ending for the Brownies. The Cardinals took the next three games with some more help from a nervous Brown defense. Sewell's boys booted four more plays in the final three games and saw the championship go to the more savvy and experienced Cardinals.

Still, it had been a remarkable year. The St. Louis Browns had nothing to be ashamed of. They had captured the only pennant in the history of the franchise—and on the last day of the season, no less. The team's struggle gave hope to legions of people in a country at war. After all, if the Browns could win a pennant, couldn't anyone?

★　★　★

Browns fans—though there still weren't many of them—began to wonder whether the 1944 season might mark a turning point. It didn't.

The next year the Browns finished third—this time only six games off the pace, as opposed to 19½ games back in their previous third-place finish in 1942. But by the time all the first-tier players returned from the war for the 1946 season, the Browns were a lost cause once again. That year they wound up in seventh, 38 games behind the revitalized Boston Red Sox.

Sensationalist entrepreneur Bill Veeck purchased the Browns in 1951 and tried to popularize the franchise by taking the novel approach of playing up its lack of talent and by staging a variety of promotional stunts. The most notorious of these was when Veeck sent midget Eddie Gaedel up to pinch hit one day. Gaedel drew a walk. It was good for a laugh. People still wouldn't come to the ballpark.

In late 1953 St. Louis and the rest of organized baseball breathed a melancholy sigh of relief when Veeck sold the Browns to a group of investors who promptly moved the team to Baltimore and renamed it the Orioles. Time passed.

In the late sixties and early seventies, the Baltimore Orioles developed an incomparable pitching staff behind stars like Jim Palmer, Mike Cuellar, and Dave McNally. Sluggers like Boog Powell and Frank Robinson supplied the offense. Skipper Earl Weaver played the best game of managerial chess in the majors. The Orioles were, at this time, the unquestioned heavyweights of the American League. And people had all but forgotten about a purported big league team called the St. Louis Browns, a team that courted forgettability like a suitor for 52 of its 53 years of existence.

But, by God, war or no war, they took the flag in '44.

CHAPTER THREE

WHIZ KIDS

THE 1950 PHILADELPHIA PHILLIES

THE YEAR BEFORE . . .

Final 1949 National League Standings

TEAM	W	L	PCT	GB
Brooklyn	97	57	.630	—
St. Louis	96	58	.623	1
Philadelphia	**81**	**73**	**.526**	**16**
Boston	75	79	.487	22
New York	73	81	.474	24
Pittsburgh	71	83	.461	26
Cincinnati	62	92	.403	35
Chicago	61	93	.396	36

"Phillies fans are so mean that one Easter Sunday, when the players staged an Easter egg hunt for their kids, the fans booed the kids who didn't find any eggs."

— BOB UECKER

In the years immediately following World War II, baseball's war casualties had returned from the front line and the game once again had slipped into a comfortable groove. The country was rebounding at last from one of its darkest periods. Optimism ruled the day.

It was considered the golden age of baseball—and specifically of New York baseball. The Yankees pretty much owned the game, entering their second generation as baseball's only true dynasty. The Brooklyn Dodgers, boasting such immortals as Gil Hodges, Jackie Robinson, Pee Wee Reese, Roy Campanella, and Don Newcombe, dominated the National League. Year after year, it seemed, the Dodgers would get to the World Series—only to succumb to the mighty Yanks.

In the late forties, the Boston Braves, New York Giants, and St. Louis Cardinals were generally the ones who rubbed elbows with Brooklyn in National League pennant races. The Braves had Warren Spahn, Johnny Sain, and Tommy Holmes. The Giants had Eddie Stanky, Alvin Dark, Sal Maglie, and Bobby Thomson. And the Cardinals boasted Enos "Country" Slaughter, Red Schoendienst, and the incomparable Stan Musial.

The Philadelphia Phillies, in stark contrast, were considered a standard-issue second division team. The last time they had won the pennant was in 1915, and they had never won a World Series. Between 1915 and 1949, the Phillies finished over the .500 mark only four times. In that same stretch of 34 seasons, they finished second-to-last on eight occasions and dead last 17 times. With the American League Philadelphia Athletics faring only slightly better during that period, Philadelphia fans, with some justification, grew bitter and disenchanted with their local teams. To this day, they are known as some of the toughest baseball fans in the country.

Things hadn't always been so bleak for baseball fans in the City of Brotherly Love. Connie Mack's Athletics had occasionally been at the top of the heap, winning the World Series in 1910, 1911, and 1913, then later in 1929 and 1930. But the 1950 Phillies had no such dynasties to point to They had simply been insignificant for thirty-plus years.

★ ★ ★

Actually, the legacy of futility had its roots in the early days of the game
In 1883, attorney/politician John Rogers got together with sporting goods mogul Alfred Reach and bought the Worcester Brown Stockings. Their plan was to bring National League baseball to Philadelphia by moving the franchise there. The two owners watched their creation, renamed the Phillies, stumble to one of the worst seasons ever posted by a professional team. Their 17-81 record that year registered a microscopic winning percentage of .173. The club improved over the next few years under the management of Harry Wright, and—while not setting the world afire—they avoided last place for the rest of the nineteenth century.

Owners Rogers and Reach parted ways in 1902; Reach sold his portion of the franchise and resigned as club president after lengthy squabbling. The breach signalled the onset of a long dark period in Philadelphia. The club lost its best player, second baseman Nap Lajoie, after his contract was bungled. To make matters worse, Lajoie signed on with the crosstown Athletics. The Phillies were able to obtain a court order barring Lajoie from playing in the state of Pennsylvania, but this only soothed management egos; the damage to the team's lineup had already been done.

The next year, Ed Delahanty—their only other superstar—left the team and subsequently died in a bizarre, drunken accident. Still more misfortune struck the Phillies when a large portion of the team's Baker Bowl bleachers collapsed during a game and killed 12 people while injuring 232. The 1903 tragedy was the worst disaster in baseball history. Attendance dwindled, as much in response to sorry play as to the spectators' fear for life and limb.

After a decade of mediocrity, things got better—for a while. The Phils—behind newly acquired pitching wizard Grover Cleveland Alexander—went to the World Series in 1915, but lost to the Boston Red Sox in five games. They contended until 1917, when Alexander was inexplicably traded.

In the 1920s and 1930s, the team plummeted and became the laughing stock of the National League. Philadelphia piled up so many last-place or next-to-last-place finishes that a sportswriter dubbed them the Phutile Phils. The nickname stuck. In 1933, the team was purchased by a debt-prone investor named Gerry Nugent who proceeded to sell off prospect after prospect to other teams for cash. This made rebuilding the team virtually impossible; as long as Nugent was in charge, the franchise seemed to have little or no hope of ever peeking out of the basement. It looked like the days of the Phutile Phils would last . . . phorever.

The National League tried to bring some semblance of professionalism to the pathetic club in 1943. Nugent was ousted; the Phillies were sold to a group of investors headed by William D. Cox. But the cure was worse than the disease: it was discovered that Cox was betting on Phillies games regularly. He was banned from baseball. The father-and-son team of Robert and Ruly Carpenter took over the franchise.

The Carpenters were serious baseball men with a genuine love for the game. They desperately wanted to create a respectable club, and they knew it would be a long and expensive process. Ruly joked, "I'm going to write a book: *How to Make a Small Fortune in Baseball*—you start with a large fortune."

One of the first things Ruly did as club president was to appoint Hall of Fame pitcher Herb Pennock to the post of general manager, with explicit instructions to develop a farm system. Though Pennock wouldn't live to see his hard work launch a new era for the franchise, his efforts would be critical to the team's success in 1950.

Less successful was a 1944 attempt to "wipe the slate clean" by renaming the team the Blue Jays. That lasted for one season.

★   ★   ★

The late forties saw some optimism arising among Phillie fans. A youth movement, soon to yield a group known as the "Whiz Kids," was gradually taking shape.

Outfield sensation Del Ennis came up through the ranks in 1946; he proved to be a solid .300 hitter with above-average power. After batting .313 in his first year, he was honored as the first *Sporting News* Rookie of the Year. Ennis hailed from Philadelphia; the local boy was immediately embraced by the usually jaded Shibe Park fans.

A kid named Dick Sisler, purchased from the St. Louis Cardinals in

1948, could play well in the outfield and at first base. He had been born in 1920, the same year his father—Hall of Famer George Sisler—had hit .407 for the St. Louis Browns. Though he never came close to hitting .400, the new Phillie could hit with moderate power and proved deadly in the clutch.

Twenty-one-year-old Richie Ashburn was promoted from Triple-A in 1948 and hit a sharp .333. The young outfielder had a keen eye, collected more than his share of walks, and could spray singles in any direction. In his first season, he nailed down the leadoff spot in the lineup. Of Ashburn, Ted Williams said, "That kid has twin motors in his pants."

Robin Roberts was a 22-year-old fireballing righthander when the Phils called him up from the Inter-State League in June of 1948. The archetypical "regular guy," Roberts often downplayed his pitching prowess by saying, "Too many people try to make it more complicated than it really is." He would go on to become the winningest righthander in Phillies history. The Robin landed in the Hall of Fame in 1976.

Teenaged lefty hurler Curt Simmons got his call at the tail end of 1947, but didn't really find his groove until the 1950 season. Similarly, shortstop Granville "Granny" Hamner was a very green 17 when the Phils called him up in 1944. He bounced between the majors and minors until 1949, when he finally nailed down the job of first-string shortstop.

First baseman Eddie Waitkus was an old-timer compared to his teammates. He was all of 30 in 1950. Considered one of the premier defensive first basemen in the game, the lanky Waitkus added a solid lefthanded bat to the lineup when the Phillies acquired him from the Chicago Cubs after the 1948 season.

Waitkus was the inspiration for Roy Hobbs, the main character in the novel and, later, the motion picture *The Natural*. In the middle of the 1949 season, he was shot in a Chicago hotel room by a deranged woman he did not know. His chest injuries were serious and he nearly died, but over the winter Waitkus toiled feverishly to rehabilitate himself in time for the following season. It was as if he knew the young team was brimming with potential; the wounded "graybeard" wanted to be there for a shot at the pennant.

★　★　★

Eddie Sawyer returned for his second full year as Phillies skipper in 1950. When he first joined the club midway through the 1948 season, the Phils were mired in sixth place. They improved the following year to third place, 16 games behind the Dodgers and Cardinals.

As the 1950 season got underway, Sawyer was excited by what he saw. Eddie Waitkus showed no signs of the freakish gunshot wound he had suffered. Shortstop Granny Hamner and second baseman Mike Goliat—who had never played second in the minors—were becoming a potent double-play combination. And 25-year-old Willie "Puddin' Head" Jones was holding down the hot corner like a seasoned veteran and hitting close to .300.

The Phillies got off to their best start in recent memory.

National League Standings: June 14, 1950

TEAM	W	L	PCT	GB
St. Louis	31	17	.646	—
Brooklyn	28	20	.583	3
Philadelphia	**27**	**20**	**.574**	**3½**

They played their hearts out, keeping pace with the Dodgers and Cardinals for the first half of the season. On several occasions before the All-Star break, the Phils were able to squeak into first place for a day or two, but with the Dodgers and Cards surging, they slipped back in the pack—as, indeed, all of baseball expected them to.

★   ★   ★

But during the last week of July, with the Cardinals suddenly skidding and the Dodgers treading water, the Whiz Kids pulled ahead of the pack. Sportswriters gave the youngsters credit for playing above their heads and overtaking the league powerhouses. Could it continue?

Through the month of August, the Phillies were able to pad their lead with surprising ease. Going into the final month of the season, the franchise was poised to win its first pennant in 35 years. A team made up primarily of inexperienced youngsters was weaving a Cinderella story for the nation.

National League Standings: September 1, 1950

TEAM	W	L	PCT	GB
Philadelphia	**78**	**47**	**.624**	—
Brooklyn	69	50	.580	6
Boston	68	54	.557	8½

Robin Roberts was having a magnificent year, and so was Simmons, but reliever Jim Konstanty was the one who truly carried the club. The bespectacled righty was, at the ripe old age of 32, one of the oldest members of the team. He was en route to the finest season of his ten-year career. By season's end, he would rack up 74 appearances, 16 relief wins, and 22 saves. His 1950 performance, more than any other factor, spelled the difference between first place and the second division for the Phillies. After the dust settled, he made history by becoming the first relief pitcher to win the Most Valuable Player Award.

National League Standings: September 18, 1950

TEAM	W	L	PCT	GB
Philadelphia	**87**	**54**	**.617**	—
Boston	78	60	.565	7½
Brooklyn	76	60	.559	8½

Just when it looked like the Whiz Kids were home free, something happened.

Perhaps they had been thinking about the pennant too much—there was certainly a lot of media pressure on the team. Or perhaps it was the physical problems: starters Bob Miller and Bubba Church suffered injuries that put them out for the rest of the year. The hurdle might have been bad luck: Curt Simmons, who was 17-8 at the time, was summoned to military duty in the middle of September; in six consecutive starts, staff ace Robin Roberts failed to notch his 20th victory. Whatever the cause, the Phillies came apart at the seams in the second half of September.

Their fans were not so much worried as surly and impatient. Even with the Phils in first place and still very close to clinching, there had been some hooting at Shibe Park, lovable youngsters or no lovable youngsters. There was—and is—a history of vitriolic behavior in Philadephia when the home team falters, which is frequently. Years later, Mike Schmidt—one of the greatest sluggers to wear a Phillies uniform—would don a day-glo fright wig on the field in an attempt to curb the fan abuse he was receiving during a batting slump. Legendary radio announcer Russ Hodges once quipped, "If Ben Franklin played shortstop here and made an error, they'd probably boo him for a week, too."

The fan abuse begat more bad play, which begat more abuse. The Whiz Kids, who were now precariously close to becoming the Fizz Kids, lost nine of twelve games, including three to the revitalized Dodgers. Brooklyn, meanwhile, won 13 of 16 contests. With their 7-3 victory over the Phils on September 30th, the Dodgers pulled within a game of first place with one game remaining on the schedule.

National League Standings: October 1, 1950

TEAM	W	L	PCT	GB
Philadelphia	**90**	**63**	**.588**	—
Brooklyn	89	64	.582	1
New York	85	70	.556	5
Boston	83	70	.542	7

After maintaining what looked like a more-than-comfortable lead over the Dodgers, the Phillies had crumbled in just two short weeks. Cynics said it was inevitable—that the young Phillie squad couldn't take the rigors of a pennant race. But the season wasn't over yet.

By a remarkable twist of scheduling, Philadelphia's last regular season game, on October 1st, pitted the Whiz Kids against the second-place Dodgers. The game would be played on Brooklyn's home turf. A Phillie win would clinch the pennant; a Brooklyn victory would force a three-game playoff series. With the way the Dodgers had been playing, Eddie Sawyer wanted to wrap the pennant up and avoid having to play Brooklyn any more than absolutely necessary.

Ebbets Field was packed with 35,073 fans that day—the biggest

Dodger crowd of the season. Robin Roberts—still in pursuit of that elusive 20th win—took to the hill against one of the game's greatest pressure-situation pitchers, Don Newcombe.

The Phillies jumped on the board first in the fifth on a handful of singles. They were leading, 1-0, in the sixth, when unlikely slugger Pee Wee Reese hit a fluke home run to right field. Reese hadn't even realized it was a homer until he had raced around third base and noticed that the ball was nowhere to be seen; it had lodged in the screen. He trotted in to tie the game at one apiece. The Brooklyn fans went crazy.

In the bottom of the ninth, with the game still deadlocked, Roberts walked Cal Abrams and surrendered a single to Reese. Abrams, not taking any chances, held up at second. The Phils expected a bunt from Duke Snider, but the future Hall of Famer lined a single into center. Richie Ashburn grabbed the ball and rifled a strike to catcher Stan Lopata; Dodger coach Milt Stock waved Cal Abrams around third. It was a bad move. Lopata had enough time to pick up a copy of the afternoon paper before the runner reached him. He easily applied the tag for the first out of the inning.

The Dodgers still looked poised to send the two teams to a playoff, though, as Reese and Snider advanced to second and third on the hit. After Jackie Robinson was intentionally walked to load the bases, Roberts caught a break when he got Carl Furillo to foul out to first on the first pitch There were now two outs with the score still tied, 1-1.

Gil Hodges, Brooklyn's biggest power threat, stepped up to the plate and sent a ball high and long to right center, but it wasn't long enough. Del Ennis hauled it in to end the Dodger threat and send the game to extra innings. Ashburn's throw and Milt Stock's fateful coaching decision loomed large.

In the top of the tenth, Roberts, in whom manager Sawyer obviously had a great deal of faith, drew a walk. Eddie Waitkus followed with a single. Ashburn tried to bunt, but Newcombe grabbed the ball and made a great play to nail the lead runner at third. Then Dick Sisler, already with three hits on the day, came to the plate to face Don Newcombe. Sisler quickly fell in the hole, 0-and-2, then lofted the next pitch sky-high to left. The left field stands at Ebbets Field were a mere 348 feet from the plate; Sisler had himself a short—but ever so sweet—three-run homer to put the Phils up by a score of 4-1.

Roberts retired the Dodgers in the bottom of the tenth and the Whiz

Kids were pennant-winners It was Roberts' 20th win of the season, he became the first Phillie to win 20 since Grover Cleveland Alexander in 1917.

After the game, Ashburn joyfully reflected on his game-saving throw. "Maybe it wasn't the best throw I made all year," he told a throng of reporters, "but I don't know of one that came at a better time."

Dodger manager Burt Shotton made his way through the crowded Phillie locker room. "Congratulations, Eddie!" he shouted to the celebrating Phillie skipper, "You did a great job. If we had to lose, I'm sure glad it was to you. Go get those Yankees now!"

Final 1950 National League Standings

TEAM	W	L	PCT	GB
Philadelphia	91	63	.591	—
Brooklyn	89	65	.578	2
New York	86	68	.558	5
Boston	83	71	.539	8
St. Louis	78	75	.510	12½
Cincinnati	66	87	.431	24½
Chicago	64	89	.418	26½
Pittsburgh	57	96	.373	33½

It had been a long time coming, and Philadelphia celebrated the young heroes. A few years earlier, veteran sportswriter Frank Yeutter had promised to give up his beloved mustache if and when the Phillies won the pennant. Now he dutifully allowed Granny Hamner and Bubba Church to shave him clean. He was sad to see his ten-year-old mustache go, he said, but the cause more than compensated for his loss.

In more ways than one, it was the end of an era for baseball in Philadelphia. At season's end, 87-year-old Connie Mack stepped down from the Philadelphia Athletics' managerial post. Sadly, Mack's team hadn't been able to keep up with its National League counterpart; the A's finished dead last, 46 games off the pace. Connie Mack had managed his team for half a century and had succeeded in bringing them nine pennants.

But now it was the A's, not the Phillies, who were the cellar-dwellers. (The A's would eventually move to Kansas City, leaving Philadephia as a one-team town. Over the years, many had pointed to the attendance problems of both teams and argued that such a shakeout was inevitable.)

★   ★   ★

The euphoric Whiz Kids still had to face baseball's strongest team, the New York Yankees, in the World Series. It would be their biggest challenge, and they would not be able to meet it. Although they had just averted catastrophe and taken the pennant in dramatic fashion, the Phils still did not have the services of three key pitchers.

Indeed, the inability to call on Bob Miller, Bubba Church, and Curt Simmons was a crushing blow. The Yankees swept the World Series in four games, winning 1-0, 2-1, 3-2, and 5-2. The games certainly weren't blowouts, but the Phils were simply outplayed by the Bronx Bombers.

But Phillie fans, for once, eased up on their boys. The Whiz Kids had done a spectacular job of playing David against Brooklyn's Goliath in 1950. It had been a year to savor, a year in which the Phillies had proved that the bad old days of owners John Rogers, Alfred Reach, Gerry Nugent, and William Cox were over at long last. The Carpenters' seven-year rebuilding process was complete; the Phillies were now a respectable team.

★   ★   ★

Behind Robin Roberts and company, the Phils finished in the first division for four of the next five years. The Dodgers and Giants, however, dominated the National League.

Not long afterwards, however, there was another descent. From 1958 to 1961, the Phillies finished in the basement. It got so bad in '61 that they set a modern major league record by losing 23 consecutive games. Not even the lowly 1962 Mets could boast such a skid. (Interestingly enough, it was the expansion of the National League in 1962 that triggered a recovery for the Phils; they finished at 81-80 for a .503 winning percentage that year and yielded last place to the expansion Mets.)

Philadephia improved still more in 1963, finishing fourth, and then came painfully close to their third pennant in 1964. On September 20th of that year, they held a 6½-game lead over the second-place St. Louis Cardinals. An infamous ten-game losing streak cost Philadelphia the flag, which went to the Cards on the final day of the season. The collapse was the harshest blow ever suffered by Philadelphia baseball fans, and it didn't do much to improve their attitude.

The Phils didn't contend again until Mike Schmidt, Steve Carlton, and Greg Luzinski came along in the mid-1970s. Philadephia won a handful of division titles before finally bringing home a pennant in 1980; they then beat a strong Kansas City Royals squad in the World Series to capture the championship that had eluded them so many times.

All told, it took the Philadelphia Phillies 32 years to win their first pennant, another 35 to win their second one, and yet another 30 for their third. For generations of Philadelphia fans, it was an agonizing 97 years before the franchise won a world championship. No other team in baseball history had to wait so long for a world championship.

Was 1980 worth the wait? For Philadelphia's long-suffering partisans—fans who, according to the ever-colorful Bo Belinsky, "would even boo a funeral"—it certainly was.

CHAPTER FOUR

MIRACLE AT COOGAN'S BLUFF

THE 1951 NEW YORK GIANTS

THE YEAR BEFORE . . .

Final 1950 National League Standings

TEAM	W	L	PCT	GB
Philadelphia	91	63	.591	—
Brooklyn	89	65	.578	2
New York	**86**	**68**	**.558**	**5**
Boston	83	71	.539	8
St. Louis	78	75	.510	12½
Cincinnati	66	87	.431	24½
Chicago	64	89	.418	26½
Pittsburgh	57	96	.373	33½

"The Giants? The Giants is dead."

— BROOKLYN DODGER MANAGER CHUCK DRESSEN

AUGUST, 1951

Prior to baseball's expansion to the West Coast in 1958, New York City boasted no fewer than three major league baseball teams. In those days New Yorkers came in three distinct varieties. You were either a Yankee fan, a Dodger fan, or a Giant fan. There was no middle ground. The team you favored said almost as much about you as your religion, and you switched allegiances with about as much frequency.

The Yankees, of course, had a certain advantage. For one, they ranked as the most successful sports franchise of all time, a position they still hold. By 1951, they had accumulated an unprecedented fourteen world championships. As of this writing, they've upped the total to twenty-two.

In the pre-1958 days, the Bronx Bombers had another edge of sorts over the other New York squads: they were the only Big Apple team in the American League, which meant they didn't have to deal with a contending local. Their closest league rivals were seemingly light-years away in remote outposts like Cleveland and Boston.

On the other side of the coin there were the New York Giants and Brooklyn Dodgers of the National League. The Giants and Dodgers had a rivalry of legendary proportions, one that dwarfed the later confrontations between the San Francisco and Los Angeles incarnations of the franchises. For decades, Manhattan dwellers and Brooklynites argued over which borough had the better team. Barroom fights would break out. Feuds would develop. Cross-town relatives would sever family ties. It all happened year after year, as the Giants and Dodgers staged their seemingly inevitable struggles for the National League flag. And, to the chagrin of Giants partisans, the Bums from Brooklyn usually triumphed.

In 1951, it had been fourteen long years since the Giants had won their last pennant in the days of "King" Carl Hubbell and Mel Ott. During those fourteen years World War II had come and gone, the Great Depression had ended, and television had begun to creep into America's living rooms. Giants fans were hungry.

They looked for salvation to an unlikely source—manager Leo "The Lip" Durocher, the former Brooklyn skipper.

★ ★ ★

Brooklyn fans had never been more shocked when, smack in the middle of the 1948 season, Durocher, a Dodger institution, accepted a job offer to manage the hated New York Giants. Dodger owner Branch Rickey had apparently had enough of the fiery Durocher's controversial style—but unloading him was a move that few Brooklyn fans could comprehend, much less forgive.

For their part, Giant fans had been less than thrilled with the move. Their own beloved manager/icon, Mel Ott, had been abruptly whisked out of the dugout and hidden away with a front-office job to make room for Durocher, a man despised for years by the Giant faithful. But Durocher had not been trying to challenge team loyalties—he was broke (a not uncommon circumstance), and he readily admitted accepting the Giants' offer purely for economic reasons.

"The Lip" had the reputation of being a bully with his troops; he was either a flamboyant, arrogant gambler or a "colorful character," depending on whom you talked to. As a player he was an outstanding defensive shortstop but a terrible hitter, playing for four teams over seventeen years. The fiercest of competitors, he once said, "If I were playing third base and my mother were rounding third with the run that was going to beat us, I'd trip her. Oh, I'd pick her up and brush her off and say, 'Sorry, Mom,' but nobody beats me." Few could match Durocher's desire to win, either as a player or as a manager. During his eight-and-a-half-year stint as Dodger skipper, he compiled a .566 winning percentage, leading the team to a pennant and three achingly close second-place finishes.

New York Times columnist Arthur Daley once related a story about Durocher that took place during the Giants' 1951 spring training in St. Petersburg. The Lip was approached in a hotel lobby by a fortune teller who wanted to read his palms. Durocher, ever the realist, flatly refused, saying, "Naw, I don't go for that sort of stuff." His wife and friends suggested that he lighten up and have a go at it. After a few minutes of goading, the suspicious manager agreed it might be worth a laugh and surrendered his palms.

"You will get off to the worst start of your managerial career this spring," the palmist told him. Durocher's grin evaporated and he almost snatched his hands away. But the soothsayer continued, ". . . and then your team will start to pick up momentum shortly after your birthday and will be going like the wind at the end." Durocher and his entourage chuckled and went their way.

★ ★ ★

On April 17, after posting a 19-12 record (with two ties) in spring training, the Giants started the season proper against the Boston Braves at Braves Field. With patches of snow still on the New England ground and the temperature quite unlike that of balmy Florida, it was a bitter way to begin the year. Only about 6,000 fans showed up for Opening Day, but those who did witnessed Giant Larry Jansen hurl a sparkling five-hit shutout. The Giants had won their opener for the first time in five years. Afterwards the uncharacteristically relaxed Leo smirked and quipped, "We probably won't lose a game all year."

They lost their first the next day. After their ace Sal "The Barber" Maglie lost his stuff (and the lead) in the sixth, the Giants staged a ninth-inning comeback to tie the Braves—but Boston slugger Sam Jethroe lined a three-run homer in the bottom of that inning to win the dramatic contest for Beantown.

The third day of the season saw Jim Hearn on the mound for New York in the first game of a doubleheader. Hearn had come over from the Cardinals in the middle of the previous season and proved nearly unhittable, going 11-3 for the Giants with a superb ERA of 1.94. That afternoon he kept the Braves at bay and the Giants went to 2 and 1 with a 4-2 victory.

It was the last Giant fans would see of the good side of .500 for a long time. New York's pitching fell apart in the nightcap and, after going through six pitchers, the Giants lost a 13-12 slugfest. New York then headed home to the Polo Grounds for a three-game series against their arch-rivals, the Dodgers—who beat them two days in a row by identical 7-3 scores. In the second game, when Dodger catcher Roy Campanella was grazed by a Larry Jansen fastball, he began screaming at Giant catcher Wes Westrum; within seconds both benches had cleared. A brawl was narrowly averted, but when the game resumed Campanella hit a double. Durocher, who had ordered Jansen to pitch Dodger batters close, could be forgiven for harboring a certain uneasy feeling. The season was only a few days old and already things were starting to look bad.

After suffering two blow-outs in a row at the hands of Brooklyn, the Giants had one more chance to notch a victory on their home turf against the hated Dodgers. And they came close, too, leading 3-1 in the eighth. But Brooklyn tied the score in the ninth and won the game in the tenth on a Carl Furillo homer. Brooklyn had *swept* the Giants at the Polo Grounds.

The broom work went on into May. The palm reader's prediction was coming true: Durocher and his Giants were off to a miserable 2-12 start, with eleven of their losses occurring consecutively. The Giants had to do something to shake things up, and they had to do it fast. The fans started getting ugly.

★ ★ ★

In the middle of May the Giants promoted one Willie Howard Mays from their Minneapolis Triple-A affiliate. As a teenager, Mays had been a sensation with the Birmingham Black Barons of the Negro League. After the notoriously racist Boston Red Sox gave Mays a cursory tryout and drafted the immortal Piper Davis instead, the Giants scouted him, liked what they saw, and snapped him up immediately. The young man had outstanding overall skills and an unbridled enthusiasm for the game. Though he hadn't spent too much time with Minneapolis, Mays tore the bush leagues apart. Giants owner Horace Stoneham went so far as to placate the Minneapolis fans by taking out an ad in the local paper apologizing for promoting the popular phenom: the twenty-year-old outfielder had been hitting a cool .477 when he got his call to the show.

Mays was uneasy about the prospect of facing major league pitching. When Durocher heard about the kid's nervousness, the manager asked him what his average had been in Minneapolis. Mays told him. Stunned, Durocher asked, "Do you think you could hit *half* that for me?"

After churning a few stomachs with an 0-for-22 start on the road, Mays was able to fill the request. In his first Polo Grounds at-bat, he homered off of the legendary Warren Spahn. As Spahn cracked after the game, "It was a perfect pitch—for the first sixty feet."

Even considering the youngster's early troubles, Durocher had a feeling Mays was something special. Durocher was later quoted in Peter Beilenson's *Grand Slams and Fumbles* as saying, "If somebody came up and hit .450, stole 100 bases and performed a miracle in the field every day

I'd still look you in the eye and say Willie was better. He could do the five things you have to do to be a superstar: hit, hit with power, run, throw, and field. And he had that other magic ingredient that turns a superstar into a super superstar. He lit up the room when he came in. He was a joy to be around."

Monte Irvin, the Giants' left fielder, roomed with Mays and agreed with Durocher. Years after the historic 1951 season, Irvin told celebrated baseball writer Donald Honig, "Leo assigned [Mays] to room with me and we became good friends. He was a fine young man, with a wonderful, happy-go-lucky disposition. No inhibitions. All he wanted to do was play ball. He was a tonic to have around, and not just for his great ability. Everybody was extremely fond of him."

With Mays gradually finding his stroke and playing as a starter in center field, New York finally started to win some games. They climbed out of the National League cellar in mid-May and cleared the .500 mark a couple of weeks later.

Still, the Giants' bats were distressingly quiet and their victory margins were awfully tight. Shortstop Alvin Dark was the only regular hitting over .300. Others hovered in the .240 range. It was the pitching that was carrying the club; without the solid work of starters Maglie, Jansen, and Jim Hearn, the Giants would have been out of the race entirely.

Durocher's team made headway in June and early July. Nearing the middle of the season, they had taken a firm grip on second place, but they still seemed unlikely to catch the surging Dodgers.

National League Standings: July 2, 1951

TEAM	W	L	PCT	GB
Brooklyn	43	25	.632	—
New York	**39**	**32**	**.549**	**5½**
St. Louis	35	32	.522	7½

It was the All-Star break. Things were under control in Brooklyn. Baseball fans were ready for another Subway Series between the Dodgers and Yankees.

★   ★   ★

The National League All-Star team was completely dominated by Brooklyn players. A total of seven ballplayers represented the Dodgers in the July 10th game at Detroit—Roy Campanella, Gil Hodges, Don Newcombe, Pee Wee Reese, Jackie Robinson, Preacher Roe, and Duke Snider—while the Giants sent only Dark, Jansen, and Maglie. The Barber won the game for the N.L., 8-3, but with Dodger uniforms peppering the N.L. All-Star squad, the Bums still seemed to have all but wrapped up the pennant.

July 27th marked Durocher's birthday and, palm reader or no palm reader, things were still quite glum around the Polo Grounds. Actually, the Giants were holding steady and playing good ball, but you wouldn't know it to listen to their fans. Although Durocher's team had held onto second place, the gap in standings between New York and Brooklyn seemed to widen daily. Duke Snider, Jackie Robinson, and Gil Hodges were slugging homers left and right, while Don Newcombe, Preacher Roe, and Carl Erskine were mystifying National League batters everywhere. In a three-game series against Brooklyn at Ebbets Field starting on August 8th, the Giants were swept again, and Durocher's season seemed to have slipped past the point of no return.

Brooklyn was simply playing magnificent baseball. The Dodgers looked to have wrapped things up by mid-August. For all intents and purposes, the regular season was over . . . or so it seemed.

National League Standings: August 11, 1951				
TEAM	W	L	PCT	GB
Brooklyn	69	34	.670	—
New York	**59**	**50**	**.541**	**13½**
Philadelphia	56	52	.519	15

It was at this point that the fortune teller's prognosis started to come true. The Giants picked up momentum shortly (well, a little over two weeks) after Durocher's birthday.

After being shut out by the Phillies in the first of a four-game series beginning August 11, the Giants took the remaining three games in a row.

They then got some sweet revenge on Brooklyn by winning three tight games—4-2, 3-1, and 2-1—from the Dodgers at the Polo Grounds.

The Giants continued their torrid pace by sweeping the Phillies, Reds, Cardinals, and Cubs to complete a sixteen-game winning streak. In just two startling weeks they were able to climb back into something resembling respectability, even if actual pennant contention was still a ways off.

After the Giants suffered a couple of tough losses, the high-flying Dodgers returned to the Polo Grounds for a two-game series. The Giants continued their revenge on Brooklyn, but this time, instead of winning close games, they pounded Brooklyn pitching, winning 8-1 and 11-2.

National League Standings: September 1, 1951

TEAM	W	L	PCT	GB
Brooklyn	82	45	.646	—
New York	**76**	**53**	**.589**	**7**
Boston	64	61	.512	17

While the Dodgers stumbled a bit on a road trip, the Giants kept winning game after game. After winning five more in a row, they took a 3-1 defeat against the Reds at Cincinnati on September 20th. It would be their last regular season loss.

In spite of the Giants' recent surge, the Dodger front office began distributing World Series ticket applications on the morning of September 21. Management's supreme confidence in their boys should have reassured Brooklyn fans. But even though thousands of applications were given out, there was an air of apprehension sweeping Flatbush. The pennant everyone had taken for granted was looking less like a certainty with every passing day.

National League Standings: September 25, 1951

TEAM	W	L	PCT	GB
Brooklyn	93	54	.633	—
New York	**92**	**58**	**.613**	**2½**
St. Louis	79	71	.527	15½

It could no longer be denied. Durocher and his Giants—13½ games back not even a month and a half earlier—were threatening to overtake the once-uncatchable Bums.

★ ★ ★

On the 25th, the Boston Braves swept a doubleheader against the Dodgers. The Giants won their game that day, and the Brooklyn lead was down to a single game.

A couple of days later, the Giants had the day off while the Braves took a heartbreaker from Dodger great Preacher Roe, 4-3. The lead was now down to a half-game. The Giants were idle again the next day—and when Brooklyn's Carl Erskine lost to the Phillies, the Giants and Dodgers were tied for first.

The next afternoon, the Giants took sole possession of first place after Maglie shut out the Braves in Boston, 3-0. In the second inning, with Warren Spahn pitching, Mays walked, stole second and third, and scored the only necessary run on a ground out. The Boston crowd—their team twenty games back—loved Willie's show. The Giants' grip on first place was fleeting, however. That evening, Brooklyn ace Don Newcombe—knowing the Giants had won a few hours earlier—bore down and pitched a masterful shutout against the Phillies to maintain the first-place deadlock.

On the final day of the season the Giants, behind Larry Jansen, edged the Braves, 3-2, and clinched—at the very least—a tie for the pennant. Bobby Thomson smashed a solo homer—his thirtieth blast of the season—while Eddy Stanky and Monte Irvin each stroked RBI singles to pace the Giants' offense.

In the visitors' clubhouse after the game, celebratory whoops and shouts turned to dead silence save for a radio tuned to Red Barber's coverage of the final Dodgers game. The Dodgers were trailing the Phillies in Philadelphia, 6-1, in the third inning—but their bats were hot and they weren't about to go away. The result of the Giants-Braves game had been posted on the Shibe Park scoreboard; it seemed to have a galvanizing effect on the Dodgers. They chipped away at the Philly lead and finally tied the game in the eighth on pinch hitter Rube Walker's two-run double.

The game went to extra innings. While the Giants listened to it on the train back to New York, Brooklyn skipper Chuck Dressen was pulling out all the stops in Philadelphia to save the Dodgers' season. He brought in every available pitcher, even an under-rested Don Newcombe. Newk gritted his teeth and protected the tie, but not before stopping a few Brooklyn hearts when he loaded the bases in the bottom of the twelfth. The game refused to end. The Giants rode on, listening and waiting with the rest of the baseball world.

Jackie Robinson, who had rescued the Dodgers all season, hit a towering home run in the top of the fourteenth to give Brooklyn a 9-8 lead. The Phillies put a man on in the bottom of the inning, but couldn't push him across. The Dodgers had won the game and preserved the first-place tie. Brooklyn fans started breathing again. The Dodgers and Giants would meet in the National League's first playoff. The next morning, the *New York Times* ran the story in huge headlines. Somewhere in Florida a palm reader was smiling.

★　★　★

National League Standings: October 1, 1951
(end of regularly scheduled games)

TEAM	W	L	PCT	GB
Brooklyn	96	58	.623	—
New York	**96**	**58**	**.623**	**—**
St. Louis	81	73	.526	15

The Dodgers had done a remarkable job to retain even a share of first place. Still, there were many who felt it should never have come to this. The race that should have been a runaway for Brooklyn was now a brand-new, three-game season, and the Bums had to face their crosstown rivals at a disadvantage: if the series went the full three games, the Giants would be supported by the partisan Polo Grounds fans for two of them.

Not that they didn't deserve it. The Giants had won 52 of their last 63 games, an .825 clip. They went an astounding 37-7 down the stretch, and they had to win their last seven games in a row to catch the Dodgers.

New York baseball fans were in a frenzy. The Yankees had coasted (relatively speaking, of course) to the American League flag. During the final two weeks of the season, they had pulled away from the pesky Cleveland Indians after being neck-and-neck for a month and a half. Whatever the outcome of the playoff, there would be yet another subway series in the Big Apple. Then as now, New Yorkers were insufferable in success—and what success!

The first playoff game was at Ebbets Field, where Jim Hearn induced ground out after ground out to keep Brooklyn's bats cool for nine innings. Hearn's only mistake was allowing a towering second-inning homer by Andy Pafko, but the Giants overcame the 1-0 deficit in the fourth on a Bobby Thomson homer and wound up winning by a score of 3-1. Brooklyn right-hander Ralph Branca took the tough loss, giving up Thomson's two-run blast. The pitcher and batter would meet again.

Flying high after the come-from-behind win, Durocher and company took their comeback show home to the Polo Grounds. They were in for a rude awakening in the second game. Under gray, damp skies, Brooklyn rookie Clem Labine pitched a gutsy shutout, holding the Giants to just six hits. Brooklyn sticks, meanwhile, connected all day. There were thirteen hits—including four home runs—off hapless New York hurlers Sheldon Jones, George Spencer and Al Corwin. The Giants were humiliated, 10-0, and the two teams were tied for first place for the final time.

$$\star \quad \star \quad \star$$

Virtually everyone was prepared for *something* remarkable on October 3rd, 1951, but no one—not even the Giants—could have predicted just what was in store. A race that couldn't have been any more breathtaking was about to end in one of baseball's greatest moments.

Durocher did what he had to do—he started his ace. Sal Maglie, along with teammate Larry Jansen, was leading the league with 23 wins. Maglie was a fierce competitor. Dressen, likewise, had to go with his top gun, workhorse Don Newcombe. At the start of the game, the overpowering Newk was second in the league with 162 strikeouts. Over the course of this final game, he would tie the Braves' Warren Spahn for the top spot.

Maglie faltered in the first inning when he walked a pair and served up a Jackie Robinson single. Brooklyn led, 1-0, but the Barber regained his cool and proceeded to mow down the Bums for the next six innings. Newcombe, meanwhile, had thrown six shutout innings before the Giants pushed across a run in the seventh to tie things up.

Maglie weakened again in the top of the eighth. He got one out, but then gave up back-to-back singles to Reese and Snider. A nightmarish wild pitch allowed Reese to score and Snider to reach third. That made it 2-1, Brooklyn. Durocher ordered an intentional walk for Robinson, but Maglie followed by giving up a single to Pafko: 3-1, Brooklyn. Billy Cox chipped in with a single of his own: 4-1, Brooklyn. Newcombe enjoyed a 1-2-3 inning in the bottom of the eighth, as did Giant reliver Jansen in the top of the ninth.

This was it.

Barring a miracle, the Dodgers were heading to Yankee Stadium the next day—and the Giants had pulled off enough miracles already. Surely this was the end of a magnificent pennant race.

Just before the bottom of the ninth, there was an announcement on the Polo Grounds' PA system: "Attention, press. Please pick up your Dodger credentials at press headquarters in the Biltmore tomorrow night." That made it just about as official as you could get. If the Giants' announcer was admitting defeat over the PA, this *had* to be the end of the line.

Then something unexpected happened. Newcombe actually showed signs of fatigue. Al Dark poked a single; Don Mueller followed with a single to right, sending the quick Dark to third. Monte Irvin fouled out to first for the inning's first out, but Whitey Lockman scorched a double to left, scoring Dark and sending Mueller to third. The score was 4-2, Dodgers. When Mueller was lifted for pinch runner Clint Hartung, Dressen made a historic pitching change.

Ralph Branca, who had lost the first playoff game a couple of days earlier on a Bobby Thomson home run, trotted in from the bullpen. The batter waiting in the box was none other than Mr. Thomson. Branca was poised either to earn a measure of revenge or to win a spot in the Goat Hall of Fame. At this point, few in the crowd noticed or cared that Branca was wearing uniform number 13.

The crowd—a mixture of Brooklyn and New York fans—was on the edge. Millions of fans who weren't lucky enough to be at the game listened to the radio play-by-play. College students huddled around the RCA console in fraternity houses. Extended families converged in living rooms. Bar patrons drank in reverent silence in order to hear each word of the announcer—a voice the listener came to know as a trusted friend, yet whose face was never seen. The legendary voices were Red Barber for the Dodgers and Russ Hodges for the Giants. Those who heard Hodges' frenzied broadcast of the final pitch of the 1951 National League season insist that, when it comes to baseball, television will never be a substitute for radio. Here is their proof:

> "Branca pitches, and Bobby Thomson takes a strike called on the inside corner. Bobby hitting at .292. He's had a single and a double, and he drove in the Giants' first run with a long fly to center. Brooklyn leads it, 4-2. Hartung down the line at third, not taking any chances. Lockman without too big a lead at second, but he'll be running like the wind if Thomson hits one. Branca throws. There's a long fly. It's gonna be . . . I believe . . . THE GIANTS WIN THE PENNANT!! THE GIANTS WIN THE PENNANT!! THE GIANTS WIN THE PENNANT!! THE GIANTS WIN THE PENNANT!! Bobby Thomson hit that into the lower deck of the left field stands. The Giants win the pennant and they're going crazy, they're going crazy. OOOHHH-WOOOHHH!! I don't believe it, I don't believe it, I will not believe it! Bobby Thomson hit a line drive into the lower deck of the left field stands and the place is going crazy . . . The Giants won it by a score of 5 to 4 and they're picking Bobby Thomson up and carrying him off the field!"

As Thomson trotted around the bases and the ecstatic crowd spilled onto the field, Dodger fans slumped as if they had been hit by poison darts. Every Brooklyn player—except for Jackie Robinson, who watched Thomson to make sure he touched every base—simply stared at the ground and walked off the field.

Durocher, standing in the third base coach's box at the time of Thomson's blast, went berserk. The 46-year-old manager suddenly became a man posessed, jumping up and down, screaming, wrestling players to the ground, stepping on Thomson's shoe (and ripping the leather) as he rounded third, and finally falling to the ground. The Lip tried to explain his exuberant reaction in his autobiography *Nice Guys Finish Last*: "People are always telling me that the biggest thrill in my life must have been watching Bobby Thomson's home run go into the bleachers. They are wrong on only two counts: (1) I didn't see it. (2) I wasn't thrilled, because I went into complete shock. The mind, I learned that day, can be a very strange and frightening thing."

Through the years, the second-guessers have asked this question over and over: Why didn't Dressen walk the red-hot Thomson? And through the years, Dressen has offered this answer over and over: "The only reason I pitched to Thomson was because Willie [Mays] was the next hitter." Fair enough.

Final 1951 National League Standings

TEAM	W	L	PCT	GB
New York	98	59	.624	—
Brooklyn	97	60	.618	1
St. Louis	81	73	.526	15½
Boston	76	78	.494	20½
Philadelphia	73	81	.474	23½
Cincinnati	68	86	.442	28½
Pittsburgh	64	90	.416	32½
Chicago	62	92	.403	34½

The Giants had no day off to collect their thoughts. The World Series would begin the next day at Yankee Stadium. The Yankees' wait was finally over.

Compared to the mayhem New York baseball had been through in the past month, the 1951 World Series was a huge letdown. How could Bobby Thomson's "shot heard 'round the world" be topped? Quite simply, it couldn't.

The Giants lost the World Series, four games to two. The Yanks outscored them (29-18), and outpitched them (1.87 team ERA vs. 4.67 team ERA). But Giants fans were happy to savor the memories of their longshot miracle-workers. They would taste world championship champagne a few years later, when Durocher and company would whip the Cleveland Indians (winners of 111 regular season games), four games to none in the '54 fall classic. But even that victory would not be quite the same. With the "Miracle at Coogan's Bluff" the Giants—and the world—had been treated to the ultimate baseball drama.

CHAPTER FIVE

THE OTHER SHOT HEARD 'ROUND THE WORLD

THE 1960 PITTSBURGH PIRATES

THE YEAR BEFORE . . .

Final 1959 National League Standings

TEAM	W	L	PCT	GB
Los Angeles	88	68	.564	—
Milwaukee	86	70	.551	2
San Francisco	83	71	.539	4
Pittsburgh	**78**	**76**	**.506**	**9**
Cincinnati	74	80	.481	13
Chicago	74	80	.481	13
St. Louis	71	83	.461	16
Philadelphia	64	90	.416	23

"I'm too happy to think."

— BILL MAZEROSKI, OCTOBER 13, 1960

Although the 1960 Pirates earned "longshot" status primarily with their heroics in that year's World Series, the story of their regular season deserves to be told here as well. The 1960 squad represented a remarkable turnaround for a franchise desperately in need of one. There are still plenty of Pirates fans who can attest that the Pittsburgh baseball scene in the 1950s was not a pretty picture.

The Pirates started off the decade in last place, finishing the 1950 season with a lackluster .373 winning percentage—pretty weak considering they boasted the potent bat of legendary slugger Ralph Kiner and the administrative skills of Branch Rickey. (More will be said later of Rickey's role in the transformation of the Pittsburgh club.) Even with such a poor finish, things went downhill from there.

In 1952, the Pittsburgh Pirates posted one of the ten worst seasons in baseball history—at least according to authors George Robinson and Charles Salzberg. In their excellent book, *On a Clear Day They Could See Seventh Place*, Robinson and Salzberg tell of a 1952 Pirate squad that rivaled the infamous 1962 Mets for sheer ineptitude on the diamond. They had a 21-game losing pitcher in Murry Dickson, and there were only two regular pitchers with an ERA under 4.00. Aside from Hall of Famer Ralph Kiner—who hit 37 homers with a .244 batting average that year—the team had nothing to speak of in the way of offense. The highest batting average posted by season's end was that of young shortstop Dick Groat, who hit .284 (but only played in 95 games).

In all, Pittsburgh won only 42, lost 112 (a horrendous .273 clip), and finished in last place—54½ games behind the pennant-winning Brooklyn Dodgers. The Bucs' longest winning streak of the year was two games.

Joe Garagiola, one of several catchers on the 1952 Pittsburgh squad, once explained, "With all our inexperienced players we got off to a slow start. We lost ten out of the first fourteen—and then had a slump."

★　★　★

In the 1930s, Branch Rickey had almost singlehandedly turned around the St. Louis Cardinals. His progressive approach, signing young prospects and developing something he called a "farm system," revolutionized baseball. Under his shrewd leadership, the Cardinals went from chumps to champions. Rickey got even better results with the Brooklyn Dodgers in the 1940s, and in 1947 he made baseball history, breaking the color barrier by signing Jackie Robinson to a Dodger contract.

When he arrived in Pittsburgh as Pirates general manager, Rickey—by now known as "The Mahatma" in baseball circles—inherited one of the weakest teams in the game. At the time, he proclaimed; "This is the greatest challenge I have faced in my more than forty years in baseball . . . Within three years the Pirates will be in a position to challenge for the pennant." But Rickey was almost 70 years old at the time, and critics reacted skeptically to his predictions, claiming that his best days were past.

Rickey sent out a crew of scouts and immediately started signing recommended young players. In so doing, he initiated the Pirates' first farm system. By 1952, the Pirates owned the rights to more than four hundred young players, many of them still in high school. The idea was that within a few years, a contending major league lineup would emerge from the hundreds of prospects.

This plan was all well and good for the future, but it did nothing to help the hapless lineup of the day. The Pirates were regarded as clowns by local fans, in part because of inept play and in part because of a certain general atmosphere of buffoonery. Manager Fred Haney, for instance, always wore a batting helmet—one of Rickey's innovations—while sitting in the dugout. (He had previously bumped his head numerous times on the low ceiling.) Whatever the reason, no one took Pittsburgh seriously. Attendance at Forbes Field was lousy, and, thanks to all the signings, the Pirates organization went deeply into debt.

Rickey's plan to rejuvenate the Pirates would be costly and would take much longer than his predicted three years. But even when he was forced to yield his post to Joe L. Brown, Rickey still believed his plan would work—eventually.

When he left, Rickey was roundly criticized for being ineffective, but his new recruitment system was in place. Gradually, the Pirates started promoting young talent through the ranks.

★ ★ ★

Manager Danny Murtaugh had been an infielder with the sorry Pirates outfits of the late 1940s and early 1950s. Murtaugh had been cut from the team in 1951 after batting .199, unable even to make it onto the roster of the appalling '52 team. However, Rickey and the Pirates kept him in the system as a minor league manager, and by 1957 he had earned a promotion to the struggling parent club.

Under Danny Murtaugh, the Bucs suffered through yet another humiliating year in 1957, finishing in a last-place tie with the Chicago Cubs. There were positive signs, however, as youngsters signed during the Rickey administration started to come up through the ranks. In 1958 the team seemed poised to deliver on Rickey's optimism; they went 84-70 and jumped all the way up to second place, eight games behind the Milwaukee Braves. Pittsburgh fans perked up, thinking that perhaps their boys might be onto something. Attendance improved slowly but surely.

But the next year was a disappointment. The Pirates sank to fourth place in the National League (though only nine games off the pace), winning just two more than they lost. This rebuilding thing, it seemed, would take longer than was first thought.

★ ★ ★

Still, by 1960, even the most pessimistic fans had to admit that the Pirates were carrying their best lineup in years. The players were young, but not inexperienced. By now, they had played together for a few seasons and had had time to get to know each other's playing instincts.

In the spring, most baseball experts predicted that the rebuilt Pirates would be in the running. But the powerful Milwaukee Braves—with the likes of Hank Aaron, Warren Spahn, and Lew Burdette—were the favorites to walk away with the National League flag.

★ ★ ★

For the first two months of the 1960 season, Murtaugh's boys battled with the San Francisco Giants for first place.

National League Standings: May 11, 1960

TEAM	W	L	PCT	GB
San Francisco	15	7	.682	—
Pittsburgh	**14**	**9**	**.609**	**1½**
Milwaukee	9	7	.583	3
Cincinnati	11	11	.500	4

In late May, the Pirates acquired veteran starter Wilmer David Mizell—better known as "Vinegar Bend" Mizell—from the St. Louis Cardinals. After retiring in 1962, Mizell would go on to a career in politics, serving as a Republican congressman in Missouri. Although the big lefty had a spotty pitching career and a history of control problems, the Bucs' acquisition of Mizell proved to be a smart move. He went 13-5 for the remainder of the season and solidified an already strong starting rotation that included Vern Law and Bob Friend.

In late June and early July, the Bucs went on a tear. The Giants, meanwhile, played poorly and dropped out of contention. For about a month, the Pirates found themselves in sole possession of first place—thanks in no small part to the performances of a pair of rapidly maturing stars. Rickey's farm system would produce some indespensable supporting players—but the two biggest heroes of the 1960 regular season would not be developed through his ranks.

A twenty-year-old outfielder named Roberto Clemente had been acquired by the Pirates from the Brooklyn Dodgers' Montreal farm team in 1954. The Puerto Rican native made it into the Pirates' lineup the next season and—although he was not an immediate standout—steadily developed into one of the team's best everyday players. By 1960, he was a full-blown star—a dangerous clutch hitter who could spray hits to all fields *and* hit for power. He'd end the season with a solid .314 average.

Shortstop Dick Groat had never played a single baseball game in the minor leagues. He had been a star basketball player at Duke University and then played pro hoop for the Fort Wayne Pistons. The Pirates snapped up the versatile athlete and promoted him to the bigs immediately. He played part of a season, then left in 1952 to serve in the Korean War. Groat returned in 1955 to become the Bucs' regular shortstop—and something of an anomaly: he was a flashy defensive shortstop who regularly hit over .300. He would go on to win the National League batting title (with a .325 average) and the Most Valuable Player award in 1960. Groat was, to put it simply, the backbone of the team.

In late July, the Pirates suffered a mini-slump and, thanks to a winning streak by the Milwaukee Braves, found their hold on first place in peril.

National League Standings: July 21, 1960				
TEAM	W	L	PCT	GB
Pittsburgh	**51**	**35**	**.593**	—
Milwaukee	49	34	.590	½
Los Angeles	45	39	.536	5
St. Louis	45	41	.523	6

But the Bucs recovered from their small slide. First baseman Dick Stuart, who would later be affectionately known as "Dr. Strangeglove" because of his erratic fielding, was smashing the ball in midsummer. He'd end the year with 23 homers and 83 RBIs in only 122 games.

Similarly, second baseman Bill Mazeroski was contributing to the Bucs' winning ways, hitting in the .270 range and turning a seemingly endless string of double plays with Dick Groat. Mazeroski had recently acquired from his teammates the nickname "No Touch" because of his quickness in turning double plays.

Just a year earlier, Mazeroski had been in Pittsburgh's doghouse. He had put on a good deal of weight, and his hitting had suffered. Mean-spirited fans blamed his problems on an overactive social life, but the real reasons for Mazeroski's poor performance in 1959 were personal: his father had recently died and he took it badly. He had shown up for spring training in 1960 fit and trim; his batting average soon climbed back to where it was supposed to be.

Big righthander Vern Law was enjoying a career year on the mound; he was on his way to 20 victories and 18 complete games. Bullpen legend Elroy Face, coming off his record-setting 1959 season (in which he won 18 games in relief with only one loss), continued to show why he was the game's premier reliever. He would end the season with 10 relief wins, a 2.90 ERA, and 24 "retroactive" saves. (Saves were not yet an official statistic in 1960.)

These outstanding individual performances were the product of Branch Rickey's "bulk purchase" of prospects just a few years earlier. By the middle of September, with the Pirates safely settled back in first place, it was hard not to conclude that Rickey's tenure with the Pirates was the reason for their current success.

National League Standings: September 16, 1960

TEAM	W	L	PCT	GB
Pittsburgh	**88**	**54**	**.614**	—
St. Louis	79	59	.572	6
Milwaukee	80	61	.567	6½
Los Angeles	76	64	.543	10

Pittsburgh had caught pennant fever for the first time in decades. Forbes Field was suddenly packed and, with the Pirates now positioned to coast to the pennant, Bucs fans could look forward to the World Series coming to town. They just weren't sure which American League club would take on the home team.

At the time, the New York Yankees, Baltimore Orioles, and Chicago White Sox were all vying for the American flag. In the third week of September the Yanks finally pulled away from the pack and ended the season with a 97-57 record, eight games ahead of the second-place Orioles.

Pittsburgh's older fans looked forward to a rematch of the 1927 World Series, and to a measure of revenge. In that fall classic, the Yankees had swept the Pirates in four games.

Final 1960 National League Standings

TEAM	W	L	PCT	GB
Pittsburgh	95	59	.617	—
Milwaukee	88	66	.571	7
St. Louis	86	68	.558	9
Los Angeles	82	72	.532	13
San Francisco	79	75	.513	16
Cincinnati	67	87	.435	28
Chicago	60	94	.390	35
Philadelphia	59	95	.383	36

If the Pirates had a score to settle with the Yanks, they were preparing for the Series with considerably less acrimony than their forebears of thirty-three years earlier. The '27 Series had been marked by a controversy stemming from Pittsburgh manager Donie Bush's refusal to play his star outfielder Kiki Cuyler. (The two had been feuding.) Moreover, the Pirates suffered severe humiliation when, in Game 4, their pitcher Johnny Miljus unleashed his second wild pitch of the ninth inning, allowing the championship-winning run to score. The '27 Yankee squad, later acknowledged by many to be the greatest in history, stood at the beginning of a dynasty. The Pirates would not appear again in the World Series until the fateful 1960 season.

While the 1960 World Series would not, by any stretch of the imagination, be brilliantly played by either team, it would be worth remembering for a long time. It would, for one thing, be one of the most statistically unusual fall classics. And it would have one of the most astounding climaxes in Series history.

★   ★   ★

In Pittsburgh, the Pirates took Game 1, 6-4, behind Vern Law's fine pitching and Bill Mazeroski's two-run homer. Law scattered ten hits, giving up only two runs before yielding to Elroy Face in the eighth. Bob Friend got the start for Pittsburgh the next day and left after four innings, trailing, 3-0.

The Pirates' usually dependable bullpen was suddenly leaking like a sieve; the Yanks jumped on everything and won the game in a walk, 16-3.

The Series moved to New York for Game 3. It was another blowout, with the Pirates on the losing end once again. Whitey Ford pitched a brilliant four-hitter and allowed no runs. The Yankees, behind a first-inning grand slam by Bobby Richardson (who had six RBIs on the day) coasted to a 10-0 shutout.

Down in the Series two games to one, Murtaugh's crew rallied together and won the next two games at Yankee Stadium by scores of 3-2 and 5-2. Back in Pittsburgh, however, they were rocked yet again by the Yankees. As in Game 3, Whitey Ford pitched a complete-game shutout, and the Yankees tortured six Pittsburgh hurlers, scoring 12 runs. Bobby Richardson set a new World Series record by knocking in his 11th and 12th runs of the Series.

The confrontation would go to a seventh and deciding game, but you would never have known it by looking at the composite box scores. With the way the Yankees' offense had been exploding, it looked very much as though New York had simply been toying with the Pirates, spotting them a few pitchers' duels to keep things interesting.

★　★　★

On October 13, 1960, a crowd of 36,683 packed Forbes Field for the climax of this bizarre, seemingly mismatched showdown. The Pirates scored first, with two runs in each of the first two innings. New York came back and scored one in the fifth and four in the sixth to take a 5-4 lead. The Bombers added some insurance in the top of the eighth. The score stood at 7-4; the Pirates were down to their final six outs. If the Yanks could hang on, it would mean an unprecedented eighth world championship in ten years.

But the Yankees were in for a shock. In the bottom of the eighth, the Pirates put together five runs on two solid singles, a freak bad-hop grounder that hit Yankee shortstop Tony Kubek in the throat (and necessitated his hospitalization), a sacrifice, an infield hit, and finally a three-run homer by Hal Smith over the left field fence. When the strange half-inning was over, the Pirates had manufactured a 9-7 lead.

The game was to get weirder.

Bob Friend, who had been having a terrible Series as a starter, came in from the bullpen to try to finish off the Yankees and bring Pittsburgh the championship. He couldn't shut the door. Friend gave up two consecutive singles, which brought the go-ahead run to the plate with no outs. Murtaugh summoned Harvey Haddix, who got Roger Maris to foul out. But then Mickey Mantle stepped up and stroked an RBI single to right center, sending Gil McDougald to third. Before Haddix could put out the fire, Yogi Berra grounded out to first, allowing McDougald to score. The game was tied, 9-9.

Ralph Terry came in from the Yankee bullpen to face Bill Mazeroski in the bottom of the ninth. Terry needed just three outs to send one of the strangest World Series games of all time into extra innings.

Maz looked at ball one; the second pitch sailed into the heart of the second baseman's strike zone. Maz connected and hit a long fly ball to deep left-center. Yogi Berra, playing left field, drifted back to the warning track, turned around, and watched the ball sail over the wall. Mazeroski had hit the only World Series-winning home run in baseball history.

Clutching his batting helmet in his hands, Mazeroski raced around the bases. He knew he needed to sprint; he had barely gotten around first base when the crazed Forbes Field crowd broke past security and spilled onto the field. Maz kept sprinting, pushing frenzied fans away left and right. He got to home plate, somehow managed to touch it, and was hauled away by his elated teammates.

Every bit as dramatic as Bobby Thomson's 1951 shot heard 'round the world, Mazeroski's home run put the cap on the Pittsburgh Pirates' remarkable championship season. With one swing of the bat, he took every sandlot slugger's fantasy and turned it into glorious reality.

★ ★ ★

Later, after things had settled down enough for him to speak civilly, Mazeroski told reporters, "I only wish my dad had been alive to see it. He was a fine ballplayer himself and was all set to get a trial with the Cleveland Indians when he lost part of his right foot in a mining accident."

The next morning the image of Bill Mazeroski leaping into the arms of his ecstatic teammates shared space on the front pages of the nation with coverage of the country's televised presidential debates. Candidates Kennedy and Nixon had a nailbiter of their own to look forward to, but the longshot Pirates had scraped, scratched, and clawed their way through a World Series against the mighty New York Yankees . . . and somehow come out on top. Pittsburgh's voters could be forgiven for considering writing in the name Mazeroski on their ballots.

Statistically, it had been one of the strangest World Series ever. The Pirates ended the Series with an awful 7.11 team ERA; the Yankees' stood at 3.54. The Yanks outscored the Pirates, 55 to 27. The Yankees set numerous records—their .338 team average for the Series is one not likely to be broken—yet they came up short where it counted. The Pirates were the champs.

★ ★ ★

"The night we won the World Series," Murtaugh later reflected with amusement, "I was understandably feeling my oats. I asked my wife how many really great managers she thought there were in baseball. Glaring at me, she said, 'I think there's one less than you do.'"

★ ★ ★

It had taken quite a while, but Branch Rickey's seemingly reckless machinations of the early 1950s finally paid off. After their world championship season, the Pirates were suddenly a powerful franchise—a franchise to be reckoned with. The team, bolstered by a solid farm system, contended throughout the 1960s and dominated the National League East during the 1970s. They enjoyed two more world championship seasons in 1971 and 1979. Only for a few years in the 1980s did Pittsburgh fall from contention: they rebounded in the early 1990s with a flurry of divisional titles and some close finishes in the playoffs—including one of the most heartbreaking losses in championship series history in 1992.

But it all went back to 1960—the year the Pirates became respectable again.

CHAPTER SIX

TO DREAM THE IMPOSSIBLE DREAM

THE 1967 BOSTON RED SOX

THE YEAR BEFORE . . .

Final 1966 American League Standings

TEAM	W	L	PCT	GB
Baltimore	97	63	.606	—
Minnesota	89	73	.549	9
Detroit	88	74	.543	10
Chicago	83	79	.512	15
Cleveland	81	81	.500	17
California	80	82	.494	18
Kansas City	74	86	.463	23
Washington	71	88	.447	25½
Boston	**72**	**90**	**.444**	**26**
New York	70	89	.440	26½

In September of 1966, the Boston Red Sox put on a little kick good enough to lift themselves out of the American League basement and finish off the season a scant half game ahead of the last-place New York Yankees. Their final record was 72-90, and they were just 26 games out of first; not bad when you consider they had played .383 ball the previous year and wound up a full 40 games behind the first-place Minnesota Twins.

If this considerable improvement was anything to cheer about, the ever-fickle (and ever-shrinking) legion of Red Sox fans weren't about to show it. New Englanders in the mid-sixties were fed up with the local team, which hadn't contended since the late forties. Ted Williams had been enjoying retirement in Florida for the better part of a decade now, Pete Runnels had quietly snagged a pair of batting titles before joining the fledgling Colt .45's, and Jackie Jensen retired because he was afraid of traveling by airplane. About the only two players around to get excited about were a couple of kids whose names were impossible to spell. But Yastrzemski and Conigliaro were bright spots on a dismal landscape.

★   ★   ★

Carl Michael Yastrzemski was a hard-hitting outfielder from Long Island who came up to the Red Sox in 1961. Relying on hard work and sheer determination rather than God-given talent, Yaz was, even early in his career, the ultimate blue-collar ballplayer. In 1963 he established himself as a minor star, winning the American League batting title by hitting .321 with 14 home runs.

Having tackled the tough job of filling Ted Williams' spikes in left field at Fenway Park, Yastrzemski was eager to play for brand-new Sox manager Dick Williams in what was thought to be the "rebuilding year" of 1967.

The other notable young Boston player was one Anthony Richard Conigliaro. The owner of one of the most graceful natural swings in the game, Tony bubbled with enthusiasm and talent. He hailed from nearby Revere, Massachusetts, and was adored by the Boston fans.

In 1965, Tony had become the youngest player ever to lead his league in home runs; he was just twenty years old when he cracked 32 dingers for the Sox that year. In 1967, Conigliaro would set another home run record by becoming the youngest major leaguer to amass 100 lifetime homers. With a swing custom-made for cozy Fenway Park, some predicted Tony C. would break Babe Ruth's record of 714 lifetime home runs. The comparisons to Ruth didn't stop there: Conigliaro was a free-spirited slugger who enjoyed and played up an image of professional glamor.

New manager Dick Williams, on the other hand, was a tough-as-nails drill sergeant of a field chief. In his 1990 autobiography, *No More Mr. Nice Guy*, Williams explained that he got his toughness from his father, who died when Williams was sixteen; as it happened, he broke his ankle on the day his father died and walked around on it for four days before having it treated. "My father would have been proud of my fortitude . . . But it was too late for that. I could only hope to carry on some of his tough traditions and spirit. Unfortunately for some weak-kneed, prima donna baseball players, I think that's what happened."

Dick Williams' gritty, no-nonsense approach to life and managing carried his triple-A Toronto club to the Governor's Cup in 1966. The Red Sox front office—seeking to apply some discipline to a team that had grown soft under the management of golf enthusiast Billy Herman—snapped him up. Williams was confident his young team would at least break .500. Oddsmakers disagreed. The folks in Las Vegas gave the '67 Red Sox a 100-1 shot at winning the American League pennant.

Williams' iron fist was felt from the first day of spring training. Sox players were suddenly required to put in long hours of conditioning under the blazing sun. A curfew was instituted and enforced. The concept of a team captain was abolished. Afternoon golf became a thing of the past. A dress code was enforced. Williams had arrived and he meant business.

As spring training continued, Williams pushed his players relentlessly to focus all of their energy on winning. He chewed them out in front of others if they were even one minute late for practice. Laps, push-ups, wind sprints, and constant hitting and fielding drills filled each day.

Williams had his pitchers play volleyball, of all things. The manager felt that instead of standing around shagging flies and gossiping during batting practice, pitchers could sharpen their competitiveness, coordination and physical condition by serving and volleying. Most everyone agreed it was a good idea . . . but Boston's springtime batting instructor and resident legend Ted Williams didn't like it. That spring Teddy Ballgame stormed out of the camp muttering under his breath, "Volleyball. Volleyball. He's got them playing *volleyball!*"

Notwithstanding the Splinter's opinion of the new routine, the Red Sox enjoyed a 14-13 spring training record—the club's best in years. A number of injuries sprang up because of the workouts' rigorous pace, however. Conigliaro suffered a cracked shoulder, Yaz strained his back, first baseman George Scott bruised his wrist, infielder Mike Andrews pulled a back muscle, outfielder Jose Tartabull suffered a pinched nerve in his leg, and several pitchers were dealing with sore arms—all before Opening Day. Still, no one appeared to be out for the season. The club, as far as anyone could tell, was still poised to attain its stated preseason goal: mediocrity.

★ ★ ★

The season did not open with much fanfare. Opening Day at Fenway Park was postponed because of winter-like weather in Boston. The temperature on April 11th was in the high thirties and there were forty-mile-an-hour gusts of wind. The climate was slightly more forgiving the next day. It was still a miserably cold, damp, gray afternoon, but the game proceeded. Boston beat the Chicago White Sox, 5-4, on the strength of shortstop Rico Petrocelli's four RBIs and Jim Lonborg's effective pitching.

After the team lost the second game, 8-5, a kid named Billy Rohr took the mound to start the season's third game against the rival Yankees in New York. It was his first appearance in the majors. The 21-year-old burned Yankee batter after Yankee batter with a mixture of mystifying pitches. He had some defensive help along the way from Yaz and George Scott, but no one could deny that Rohr owned Yankee Stadium that day.

With two outs in the bottom of the ninth, Rohr had not allowed a hit. Veteran Yankee backstop Elston Howard—who later that season would become a member of the Red Sox—stood in and lined a 3-and-2 curveball to right field to break up the rookie's no-hit bid. Yankee fans booed their own catcher.

Rohr immediately notched the game's final out, and the Red Sox won, 3-0. The kid had come within one strike of becoming the first pitcher to toss a no-hitter in his major league debut. After the game, Rohr quipped, "Sure I'm a little disappointed, but [Elston Howard] gets paid more to hit than I do to pitch, so I guess he should get one."

American League Standings: April 30, 1967

TEAM	W	L	PCT	GB
Detroit	10	6	.625	—
New York	9	6	.600	½
Boston	**8**	**6**	**.571**	**1**
Chicago	9	7	.563	1

At the end of April, Boston found itself one game out of first. But the season was quite young, and May began badly for the Red Sox. They started by losing nine out of eleven, dipping below .500 by the middle of the month. An enraged Williams simply benched players who were not producing—including Carl Yastrzemski. "If he isn't hitting, he isn't playing," the skipper barked to reporters. But it wasn't just Yaz. Boston pitching, batting, and defense were mired in nasty slumps.

Starting with a Lonborg victory on the 19th, however, things began turning around. Conigliaro, Petrocelli and Yaz came alive and joined the ranks of the league's top ten hitters. Yastrzemski had 10 home runs, third-best in the league, and Lonborg was 6-1 by month's end. The Sox won nine of thirteen games in the second half of the month and clawed their way into the young pennant race.

American League Standings: May 31, 1967

TEAM	W	L	PCT	GB
Detroit	26	15	.634	—
Chicago	25	15	.625	½
Boston	**22**	**20**	**.524**	**4½**
Cleveland	21	20	.512	5

Williams had shaken things up; the team had a healthy fear of its manager, and they became truly hungry for a shot at the pennant. Perhaps more important, the Red Sox front office realized its team had a legitimate chance at contending and responded accordingly. They bolstered the roster by acquiring pitcher Gary Bell from the Indians and utility infielder Jerry Adair from the White Sox. No one knew it at the time, but these two players would prove invaluable down the stretch. The Sox played .512 ball before snagging Bell and Adair; they would play at a .588 clip after the two joined the club.

During June and early July, however, the Sox struggled. The front-running Chicago White Sox were tough; Boston couldn't quite get within striking distance of them. On July 9, the Red Sox were in fourth place—six games behind Chicago. Only a few months earlier, very few thought the Red Sox would be so close at such an advanced stage of the season. But Williams and his crew of go-getters had no patience for cynics; they had to keep scraping out wins if they had any hopes of getting a shot at the pennant.

Their shot came right after the All-Star break. After splitting a doubleheader with Baltimore on July 13, the Red Sox went on a tear. They won ten games in a row (six of them on the road) and 14 of 16. Boston hadn't won so many consecutive games in a decade.

The streak brought the Red Sox into the thick of a frenzied pennant race; on July 22, they were just a half-game behind the White Sox.

American League Standings: July 22, 1967

TEAM	W	L	PCT	GB
Chicago	51	40	.560	—
Boston	**50**	**40**	**.556**	½
Detroit	49	42	.538	2
Minnesota	49	42	.538	2

An already tense three-team race had turned into a foursome, with the Red Sox the unlikeliest members of the party. Ears perked up all around New England. Attendance at Fenway soared.

Number-one starter Lonborg, on his way to the first Cy Young award season by a Red Sox hurler, was throwing smoke and carrying the day. By July 23rd, when the Sox finished their ten-game win streak, Lonborg was 14-3 and showed no signs of fatigue.

Though Lonborg was the standout of the staff, he certainly hadn't been the only effective pitcher. The usually-obscure Lee Stange went 5-0 in July. Recently-acquired veteran Gary Bell won 12 games after June. Relief specialist John Wyatt came out of the woodwork to win 10 and save 20. And Jose Santiago found a groove to finish the year at 12-4 with a 3.60 ERA.

While the staff ERA, at 3.36, was only average for that year, the Sox made up for it with their run production. Boston would score 722 runs in 1967—39 more than their closest competition in the A.L. Yaz, en route to a historic Triple Crown season, would swat 44 of the team's league-leading 158 round-trippers.

American League Standings: August 8, 1967

TEAM	W	L	PCT	GB
Chicago	59	45	.567	—
Minnesota	58	49	.542	2½
Boston	**58**	**50**	**.537**	**3**
Detroit	58	50	.537	3

Tragedy struck the surging Sox on August 18. In a night game against the California Angels, pitcher Jack Hamilton hit Tony Conigliaro in the left eye with a fastball. In his autobiography *Seeing It Through*, Conigliaro remembered the infamous event.

"The ball came sailing right toward my chin. Normally, a hitter can just jerk his head back a fraction and the ball will buzz right by. But this pitch seemed to follow me in. I know I didn't freeze, I definitely made a move to get out of the way of the ball. In fact, I jerked my head back so hard that my helmet flipped off just before impact."

Tony C. went down like a sack of potatoes and was rushed to the Sancta Maria Hospital across the Charles River in Cambridge. During Conigliaro's stay at Sancta Maria, a worried Hamilton tried to visit on several occasions, but was denied access. The hard-throwing Angel pitcher was thought to have tossed a spitball. If he threw at Conigliaro intentionally, perhaps trying for a little retribution for Tony's earlier single, Hamilton had reason to regret it. He knocked Tony C. out of baseball for over a year and nearly ended his life.

Conigliaro lost all vision in his left eye. He would miss the entire 1968 campaign. Eventually he made an incredible—albeit short-lived—comeback, smashing 20 homers in 1969 and an astonishing 36 in 1970. But the seemingly magical recovery soon fizzled and local boy Tony C. was out of baseball by 1972. (A side note: Tragedy continued to follow Conigliaro when he suffered a paralyzing heart attack—not related to the beaning—in 1982 and died of related complications in February of 1990. There was talk of retiring his uniform number 25, but the idea was lost in the shuffle.)

To fill the gap during Tony C's absence for the rest of the 1967 pennant race, the Sox plucked Ken "Hawk" Harrelson from the Kansas City Athletics. Harrelson had just become a free agent after a tussle with A's owner and noted curmudgeon Charles O. Finley. Charlie O. was gaining notoriety by the minute for his constant, seemingly pointless feuds with players and managers. Allegedly, he released Harrelson shortly after the slugger announced that "Charlie O. Finley is a menace to baseball." Even in 1967, this was not exactly a state secret.

The Sox outbid seven other teams by offering Hawk a $73,000 signing bonus. With their young slugger gone, the front office wasn't in the mood to take any chances. They needed a first-class replacement, and they got him in Hawk Harrelson.

Like the man he replaced, Hawk was a free-spirited, free-swinging hitter. Unlike Conigliaro, however, Harrelson could play first base as well as the outfield. Perhaps the first major leaguer to grow his hair long and wear love beads, Harrelson became known for entertaining Hollywood celebrities at his hip "pad." He boasted of spending most of his generous paycheck on his wardrobe. Hawk's flamboyant lifestyle clashed loudly with that of headstrong Dick Williams, but this was nothing revolutionary—Conigliaro had never gotten along with the manager either.

Harrelson summed up his baseball philosophy thus: "When you're doing it, when you're hitting home runs, you can get away with anything. But when you're not delivering, it won't work. They don't buy your act."

They bought his act. Hawk was an immediate hit with the fans; he was able to fill Conigliaro's patent-leather shoes nicely for the remainder of 1967, and, for that matter, the next year. (Harrelson led the league with 109 RBIs in 1968.)

★ ★ ★

In August, as the Minnesota Twins got hot, the Red Sox, White Sox and Tigers all started to slump. The result was that all four contending teams were now closer than ever.

American League Standings: August 22, 1967

TEAM	W	L	PCT	GB
Chicago	68	53	.562	—
Boston	**69**	**54**	**.561**	—
Minnesota	67	54	.554	1
Detroit	68	55	.553	1

The American League drew up plans for a four-way round-robin playoff series, in case the season ended in complete gridlock. Each team began printing World Series tickets.

American League Standings: September 6, 1967

TEAM	W	L	PCT	GB
Chicago	78	61	.561	—
Minnesota	78	61	.561	—
Boston	**79**	**62**	**.560**	—
Detroit	79	62	.560	—

The first-place tie trend continued. All the teams—except the White Sox, who lost a handful of games but bounced back with a five-game winning streak—stayed within a game of one another over the next week and a half.

When he beat the Twins, 5-4, on September 12th, Lonborg became the first Red Sox pitcher to win 20 games since Bill Monbouquette in 1963. During the game, Lonborg—wielding the bat as deftly as the ball—cracked an RBI triple and scored a key run.

Still, no single team could pull away from the pack. It was as if the four teams were locked in some intricate, ritualized dance—a dance they wanted to prolong indefinitely.

American League Standings: September 18, 1967

TEAM	W	L	PCT .	GB
Boston	**85**	**66**	**.563**	—
Detroit	85	66	.563	—
Minnesota	85	66	.563	—
Chicago	85	67	.559	½

How were the Red Sox doing it? How were last year's doormats going stride-for-stride with the top teams in the league? In September, the answer had three letters: Y-A-Z.

In the 1970s, Reggie Jackson may have earned the moniker "Mr. October," but down the stretch in 1967, Carl Yastrzemski was incomparable in the role of "Mr. September." In the final twelve games, Yaz went 23 for 44 (a scorching .523 average), hit five homers, scored 14 runs, knocked in 16, and made countless game-saving catches in left field. His every hit, it seemed, either tied a game in the late innings, brought Boston back into a game, or knocked in the winning run.

Dick Williams called Yastrzemski's season "baseball's best ever." Considering Yaz's performance in the clutch—which, at the time, was more of an issue than his winning the Triple Crown—it's hard to argue with Williams. Suffice it to say that Yaz did not carry the Red Sox during the stretch; he *was* the Red Sox.

Nevertheless, going into the final week of the season, it was still anyone's flag.

American League Standings: September 30, 1967

TEAM	W	L	PCT	GB
Boston	**91**	**70**	**.565**	—
Minnesota	91	70	.565	—
Detroit	90	70	.562	½
Chicago	89	72	.553	2

It all came down to a single day, perhaps the most intense day of baseball ever if you were a fan of Boston, Minnesota, or Detroit. With the White Sox no longer a factor (they were mathematically eliminated a day earlier after suffering a double-header sweep at the hands of the last-place Kansas City Athletics) the Red Sox faced their first-place partner Twins on the final afternoon of the regular season. The Tigers needed to sweep their double-header against the California Angels that day in order to clinch a first-place tie with the winner of the Minnesota-Boston game.

Minnesota hurler Dean Chance had a 2-0 lead going into the seventh. But Lonborg, amazingly, shook things up again as a hitter. He led off the Boston seventh with a bunt single that surprised everyone in the park but Dick Williams. Jerry Adair and Dalton Jones followed with back-to-back singles that loaded the bases for the seemingly unstoppable Yastrzemski. Yaz continued his murderous pace by lashing a two-run single to center field. When Harrelson grounded to short, Zoilo Versalles unwisely opted to throw to the plate. Jones beat the throw for the go-ahead run. Two wild pitches by reliever Al Worthington and an error by first baseman Harmon Killebrew made the score 5-2, Boston.

Minnesota nearly tied things up in the top of the eighth. With two out and two men on base, Bobby Allison scorched a base hit into the left-field corner—knocking in a run—but was thrown out at second as Yaz pulled the unlikely move of firing the ball to second instead of home. The inning was over and the threat had passed.

Yastrzemski's alert defense ultimately spelled victory for the Sox. Lonborg finished off the Twins in the ninth with a double play ball and a pop up to Petrocelli at short.

Fans poured onto the Fenway grass, hoisted Lonborg high in the air and carried him around the field. By the time he made it to the clubhouse, his uniform was shredded beyond recognition. His exuberant teammates greeted him with cascades of beer and shaving cream.

But the season was not yet over: Detroit still had to finish its doubleheader in California. The Tigers had taken the first game, 6-4, and were winning the second, 3-1, in the second inning. If they could hang on to their lead, they would meet the Red Sox the next day for a single-game playoff to decide the pennant. The radio broadcast was relayed from the West Coast to scores of New England stations. Millions of the Red Sox faithful sat glued to their radios, hoping for one last miracle. They got it. With the help of a key Don Mincher home run, the Angels rallied to win the game, 8-5. The waiting was over.

The Red Sox were American League champions.

Longtime Red Sox owner Tom Yawkey, who had purchased the team in 1933 and had dreamed of owning a world champion ever since, raised his champagne glass to Dick Williams. The owner had not consumed a drop of liquor in years due to his failing health, but he said to Williams through tears of joy, "I will drink to you."

The fiery manager softened his hard edge for a moment and responded, "Here's to you, sir, for giving me the opportunity."

Final 1967 American League Standings

TEAM	W	L	PCT	GB
Boston	92	70	.568	—
Minnesota	91	71	.562	1
Detroit	91	71	.562	1
Chicago	89	73	.549	3
California	84	77	.522	7½
Washington	76	85	.472	15½
Baltimore	76	85	.472	15½
Cleveland	75	87	.463	17
New York	72	90	.444	20
Kansas City	62	99	.385	29½

The scrappy Red Sox were the underdogs in the World Series. Their opponents, the St. Louis Cardinals, had easily clinched the National League pennant a full week before the Sox finished their season. Ending the season with 101 wins and 60 losses, the Cards were a team richly stocked with talent: slugger Orlando Cepeda, speedster Lou Brock, and singles-sprayer Curt Flood led the St. Louis offense, while the pitching staff boasted such stars as Nellie Briles, Dick Hughes, Steve Carlton, and Bob Gibson. The legendary Gibson had missed almost half the season with a broken leg, yet he still managed to go 13-7 with a 2.98 ERA.

But instead of a rout, this contest was a Series for the ages. The Cards squeaked by the Sox, 2-1, at Fenway in Game 1. Lonborg pitched a brilliant one-hitter in Game 2 and a three-hitter in Game 5; Yaz had a series average of .400 with three homers; third baseman Dalton Jones hit .389.

But Williams' kids could not continue to dream the impossible dream. Bob Gibson was untouchable, allowing only three earned runs and accounting for three of the Cards' four victories. Brock hit .414 and set a new World Series record by stealing seven bases. The Red Sox came up short and lost a memorable World Series, four games to three.

The squad became known as the Impossible Dream team, after the song from Broadway's *Man of La Mancha*. The name fit, not least because there has always been something of Don Quixote to the Boston franchise and its fans. The 1967 season proved that there was a dream worth dreaming again . . . and if it didn't come true in the end, well, Don Quixote never quite realized all of his aspirations, either.

The Impossible Dream drama signaled a new era for the club. Before the '67 Red Sox, no other major league team had jumped from ninth place to the pennant in just one season. More importantly, after the 1967 season—though there wouldn't be too many pennants for them—the Red Sox were consistent contenders. There would be few sub-.500 Red Sox teams over the next two and a half decades.

★ ★ ★

Epilogue: The Red Sox hadn't finished above .500 since 1958. The team yearbook—compiled and published nine months before the season's thrilling conclusion—had a full-page advertisement for Narragansett Beer displayed prominently on the back cover. The bold headline on that ad proclaimed, "This is the Year." No one put much faith in the laughably optimistic ad copy at the time—perhaps not even its writer. But it was an idea worth trying on for size, just in case. Since then, Boston fans have dared to hope, often against their better judgment. And baseball—if not the tattered heart of the Red Sox fan—has been better for it.

CHAPTER SEVEN

MIRACLE OF MIRACLES

THE 1969 NEW YORK METS

THE YEAR BEFORE . . .

Final 1968 National League Standings

TEAM	W	L	PCT	GB
St. Louis	97	65	.599	—
San Francisco	88	74	.543	9
Chicago	84	78	.519	13
Cincinnati	83	79	.512	14
Atlanta	81	81	.500	16
Pittsburgh	80	82	.494	17
Philadelphia	76	86	.469	21
Los Angeles	76	86	.469	21
New York	**73**	**89**	**.451**	**24**
Houston	72	90	.444	25

> *"The last miracle I performed was the 1969
> Mets. Before that you have to go back to
> Moses."*
>
> — **GEORGE BURNS**
> **IN THE TITLE ROLE OF THE FILM "OH, GOD!"**

Extraordinary events marked the summer of 1969. Chappaquiddick abruptly altered the Kennedy image. Hundreds of thousands convened in the name of music and peace at Woodstock. The president of France resigned. Vietnam raged. A man walked on the moon. And then there were the Mets.

The 1969 New York Mets are *the* biggest longshots of all time. Period. Okay, maybe not statistically or logically, but where it counts: in the hearts of anyone following baseball over the last fifty years.

The Browns and Braves had their moments in the sun, but one need only mention the words "longshot" or "miracle" in conjunction with baseball for the '69 Mets to dominate the conversation. There's good reason for this.

The New York Mets began as a franchise that represented ineptitude, humiliation, and defeat to hundreds of thousands of baseball fans. In the team's charter season of 1962, they set a modern major-league record by losing 120 games. To this day, no team has approached this standard for futility.

The '62 season has since taken on a nearly legendary status. Even showing up for Opening Day presented a problem for a number of Mets players; they were stranded in a hotel elevator the night before the franchise's debut. They made it to the game, losing by a score of 11-4. It was downhill from there. As the season wore on, each game became a showcase in how not to play the game of baseball. The Mets finished the season with an appalling .967 fielding percentage, far and away the worst in the league. They never won more than three games in a row; at one point they lost 17 consecutive games. The team boasted two pitchers with more than twenty losses apiece and two others who suffered 17 or more defeats. They finished their charter campaign in high style when third-string catcher Joe Pignatano hit into a triple play in the eighth inning of their final game. It was an awful year on the field from beginning to end.

Manager Casey Stengel admitted during the season that his crew was a bunch of frauds. "We're cheating the public," he said. He had ample evidence to support the idea that the team had betrayed its fans.

But had they really? The '62 Mets had a certain strange appeal to New Yorkers. The average person—even if he or she didn't actually enjoy watching the team—could at least identify with them. They were, clearly, a team comprised of real human beings with real feelings. In his hilarious book *Can't Anyone Here Play This Game?* Jimmy Breslin summed up the early Met mystique nicely:

> This is a team for the cab driver who gets held up and the guy who loses out on a promotion because he didn't maneuver himself to lunch with the boss enough. It is the team for every guy who has to get out of bed in the morning and go to work for short money on a job he does not like. And it is the team for every woman who looks up ten years later and sees her husband eating dinner in a T-shirt and wonders how the hell she ever let this guy talk her into getting married.

Though the Mets were a franchise that almost instantly became synonymous with losing, New York baseball fans—starved for a National League counterpart to the Yankees since the Giants and Dodgers abandoned the town in the fifties—nevertheless took the Mets to heart. The Mets became known as a gang of "lovable losers," inventing new ways to blow games almost daily. Fans flocked to the Polo Grounds (and, starting in 1964, Shea Stadium) to see immortals like "Marvelous" Marv Throneberry, Jim Hickman, Elio Chacon, and Choo Choo Coleman bumble their way through inning after sorry inning.

Taking in a Mets game also afforded fans the chance to see a few old-timers limp through the winter of their careers, since the team gave new life to some washed-up veterans. An occasionally bizarre assortment of aging stars, including Duke Snider, Frank Thomas, Richie Ashburn, Don Zimmer, and Gil Hodges ambled in and out of the Mets dugout.

Attendance, publicity, and popularity, to the surprise of many, were not problems for the Mets. The cross-town Yankees had been in decline since their last world championship in 1962 and the Mets actually managed to steal some Yankee spectators. By 1966, the Yanks drew a post-World War II franchise low of 1,124,648 people to their games; that same year the 66-95 Mets crammed nearly two million into Shea Stadium.

Everything except winning baseball games proved easy for the new kids on the block. As bad as the Mets were in 1962, they didn't get much better in the seasons that followed. Between 1962 and 1968, the team posted 100 losses or more five times. But the fans kept coming.

The Mets were cute, they were lovable, they were even fun in some strange way. But the Mets were not contenders. They were not a "real" baseball team.

Or were they?

★ ★ ★

After a 1962 campaign in which he batted .252 and hit the first homer in Mets history, Gil Hodges hung up his playing spikes early in the next season. The Mets had just traded him to the American League Washington Senators for Jimmy Piersall. Hodges was pushing forty. The Senators—themselves no strangers to last place and desperate for some new blood—made him manager. The change did the Senators no good; they posted the league's worst record in 1963. Although Hodges would remain Washington's skipper for another four years, he could do no better than a sixth-place finish in 1967. He considered getting out of the game altogether.

But the following year he was involved in another strange trade. The Mets wanted him back. New York sent righthander Bill Denehy (who was 1-7 with a 4.67 ERA in 1967) and an unspecified amount of cash to the Senators in exchange for the manager, still quite popular in New York.

The team Hodges inherited was not much better than the one he left. Casey Stengel had skippered the team to three consecutive last-place finishes and Wes Westrum, who took the managerial reins from Stengel in 1965, had racked up a frightful winning percentage of .375 in two and a half years. Any change was worth a try—and Hodges, who had been obtained at little expense, brought a certain marquee appeal.

When he arrived in New York, Hodges was asked what kind of a manager he planned to be for the Mets. His reply was to the point: "There are only two kinds of managers: winning managers and ex-managers." As it turned out, Hodges was a winning manager—by Mets standards. He got some life out of the 1968 team, which, although it finished in ninth, one game above the last-place Houston Astros, was much improved. For the first time, the Mets were within sight of .500 at season's end: they won 73 and lost 89 for a comparatively respectable winning percentage of .451. Despite the fact that Hodges suffered a mild heart attack in late September, it was the best year in the history of the franchise.

New York's offense was certainly not the reason for their marked improvement in 1968. The team hit a collective .228 that year—worst in the National League. It was the young pitching staff that seemed, well, oddly proficient. A 23-year-old Tom Seaver went 16-12 with a 2.20 ERA while lefty Jerry Koosman, 25, did even better, posting a 19-12 record with a 2.08 ERA en route to being named the N.L. Rookie Pitcher of the Year. A second-year fireballer named Nolan Ryan was effective in a starting role as well as out of the bullpen. Although Ryan had control problems in those days, he boasted the most vicious fastball in recent memory. The Mets' team ERA of 2.72 ranking fourth in the National League in 1968.

Although Koosman posted better numbers in 1968, it was the presence of the affable young Seaver that seemed to change the team's outlook. Seaver was the first player to wear a Mets uniform who refused to buy into the "lovable losers" image. The idea that there was something charming about losing disgusted him, and he made sure his teammates knew it.

Seaver had arrived in New York in a most unusual way. In 1966, while he was still enrolled at USC, the Atlanta Braves offered him $40,000 to sign with them. Seaver was about to sign on the dotted line when baseball commissioner William Eckert vetoed the deal and ruled that Seaver could sign with any team that matched the Braves' offer. As it turned out, three teams—the Indians, Phillies, and Mets—matched the offer and a lottery was arranged at the commissioner's office. The Mets' name was drawn from a hat and Seaver packed his bags for New York.

It didn't take long for him to make his presence felt. Seaver began a Hall of Fame career by winning the 1967 Rookie of the Year award. He would carry the New York Mets for a full decade. Because of his steadiness, longevity and ability to carry the club, he was eventually dubbed "The Franchise."

Armed with a more-than-promising young pitching staff and some largely unproven bats, Gil Hodges approached the 1969 season with one lofty goal for his team: to finish above the .500 mark for the first time.

★　★　★

A few days before the 1969 baseball season commenced, Arthur Daley made his annual pennant predictions in the *New York Times*. After admitting that the odds of making completely correct predictions at the start of a season were roughly 100,000 to 1, the respected columnist picked the St. Louis Cardinals to run away with the National League East title. The East, he wrote, "is the personal property of the St. Louis Cardinals, perhaps the best and deepest ball club . . . It is impossible to pick against them."

Interestingly, Daley went on to predict the Mets to finish third in the Eastern division, though almost by default. A brand new expansion team—the Montreal Expos—and a number of injury-laden squads appeared to lower the level of competition in the Mets' territory. "It's hard to believe," he wrote, "but this process of elimination seems to have advanced the Mets to third. It is to be hoped that they don't become giddy in so unaccustomed a high altitude . . . The Shea Stadium tenants could be a pleasant surprise." Daley's colleague, Joe Durso, wasn't so optimistic, predicting a fourth-place finish for the Mets. Casual fans were no doubt amused at these generous predictions. The Mets had been the butt of so many jokes for so long that a last-place finish was still considered par for the course.

Optimism of any kind did seem unwarranted given the strength of the Cardinals. The St. Louis Club had taken the 1967 World Series from the "Impossible Dream" Red Sox; they had dropped the World Series the next year to the pitching-heavy Detroit Tigers, but they still had top-drawer players like Bob Gibson, Lou Brock, Steve Carlton, and Curt Flood, and they had just acquired star first baseman-catcher Joe Torre from the Atlanta Braves. With everyone healthy and rested, manager Red Schoendienst and his crew seemed poised to reclaim the world championship.

On April 4th, as spring training ended, the *New York Times* ran a headline: "Mets Crush Cardinals, 5 to 0, and Break Camp Optimistically." Perhaps, but Mets fans probably had a good chuckle when they read this. After all, the Cardinals were arguably the best team in baseball and the Mets—no matter how much you loved them—were still the Mets.

★　★　★

In the first month of the 1969 season the New York Mets undertook a bruising battle with the expansion Montreal Expos for the rights to last place. It was a seesaw affair. As in 1968, the pitching was more than ade-quate, but manager Gil Hodges was still having trouble getting anything out of his hitters. Hodges told the media his lineup would come around.

In truth, the offensive roster was a shambles. Hodges had a handful of men who could do one or two things fairly well, but he had few depend-able all-around players. Utility men Al Weis and Ed Charles had decent gloves, but were pathetic at the plate. There were two competent first base-men (Donn Clendenon and Ed Kranepool), a gaggle of other infielders (mostly of the "utility/good-field-no-hit" variety), and at least six outfield-ers of varying levels of competence vying for a regular spot in the lineup. Catcher Jerry Grote was the only Met who seemed to have gained sole possession of his position—but then again, even he had batted an anemic .195 in 120 games in 1967.

Rather than try to end the chaos, Hodges decided to harness it. He took inventory of his troops and concluded that his only option was to wring every ounce of run production he could from his marginal hitters. He platooned just about everyone, made defensive changes when the situ-ation called for it, and seemed willing to send in pinch hitters during any inning. The fans almost never saw the same starting lineup two games in a row.

A funny thing happened: the Mets started winning ballgames. They emerged from the basement, spent May in third place, and rapidly ap-proached the coveted .500 mark. The team at the top of the heap was not, surprisingly, the Cardinals. It was Leo Durocher's Chicago Cubs. St. Louis had been victimized by a costly series of slumps and injuries and would not contend for the rest of the season.

National League East Standings: May 31, 1969

TEAM	W	L	PCT	GB
Chicago	32	16	.667	—
Pittsburgh	24	23	.511	7½
New York	**21**	**23**	**.477**	**9**
St. Louis	21	25	.457	10

By early June the Mets had strung together enough wins to pass Pittsburgh and take second place. The season was quickly approaching the All-Star break; the Mets were solidifying their hold on second. Fans and sportswriters started to wonder what was going on.

Not that anyone was foolish enough to start talking about a pennant. Durocher's Cubs kept right on winning, and the Mets couldn't seem to get within striking distance. Chicago was steeped in talent, boasting such players as Ernie Banks, Billy Williams, Ron Santo, Ferguson Jenkins, Bill Hands, and Don Kessinger. It was far and away the best Cubs squad in a generation and, with the Cardinals out of the way, it looked like Windy City fans would get their first flag since 1945. Durocher, who led the Giants during their miracle drive of 1951, knew a thing or two about New York longshots. The last thing he wanted to do was to let the Mets get close.

National League East Standings: June 30, 1969

TEAM	W	L	PCT	GB
Chicago	49	27	.645	—
New York	**40**	**32**	**.556**	**7**
Pittsburgh	38	38	.500	11
St. Louis	35	41	.461	14

So the Mets were in second place as the season's first half drew to a close, but pennant fever wasn't exactly sweeping New York City. Mets fans were astonished and delighted by the team's performance, but they were realistic nonetheless. Second place was fine.

In his classic volume *The Summer Game*, author Roger Angell reports seeing a Shea Stadium banner that read:

M is for Mighty
E is for Exciting
T is for Terrific
S is for So Lovable

Mighty, exciting, terrific, and so lovable: yes. Pennant winners' maybe next year.

★ ★ ★

On July 8, the Mets took on the front-running Cubs at Shea Stadium for the first of a three-game series. Jerry Koosman tossed a splendid game but found his team down 3-1 going into the bottom of the ninth. Chicago pitcher Ferguson Jenkins had been murder on New York batters all afternoon and was three outs from widening the Cubs' lead in the standings. But a couple of misplayed fly balls, a walk, and clutch hits by Cleon Jones and Ed Kranepool yielded a dramatic 4-3 victory for New York. Shea Stadium was beside itself.

The victory seemed to mark a turning point in the season. The Mets gained a game in the standings, of course, but they also established an important psychological edge. The Mets, once the doormat of the National League, could hold their own with the division leaders.

After the game, Cub third baseman Ron Santo huffed to reporters, "It's ridiculous. There's no way the Mets can beat us. Just no way. It's a shame losing to an infield like that . . . I wouldn't let that infield play in Tacoma."

The ball was rolling.

National League East Standings: July 9, 1969				
TEAM	W	L	PCT	GB
Chicago	52	32	.619	—
New York	**46**	**34**	**.575**	**4**
St. Louis	41	44	.482	11½
Pittsburgh	39	43	.476	12

Around this time Jimmy "The Greek" Snyder, the famed Las Vegas oddsmaker, posted his annual mid-season predictions. The Cubs, he said, had 1-to-3 odds of winning the pennant and the Mets stood at 3-to-1. At the beginning of the season, most oddsmakers had considered the Mets to be 100-to-1 underdogs. A lot can happen in four months.

The next day 59,083 people, the largest crowd in Mets history, packed Shea Stadium to watch Tom Seaver try to make it two in a row over the Cubbies. The standing-room-only crowd was seven deep in the aisles.

The record crowd was in for a treat: Seaver was incandescent that evening. He pitched eight innings of perfect baseball. Finally, with one out in the ninth and the Mets leading 4-0, he surrendered a single to Jim Qualls, a rookie hitting .243. The crowd booed Qualls mercilessly; Seaver quickly retired the final two Cubs to wrap up a brilliant one-hit victory. The Mets were within three games of first place.

After the game, a tearful and emotionally drained Nancy Seaver greeted her husband. The pitcher saw her and said, "What are you crying for? We won, 4-0!"

Later, an exuberant Ed Kranepool quipped to reporters, "It would be great to go into Chicago the last two games of the season with a three-game lead and tell Ernie Banks, 'It's a great day to play two, Ernie.'"

The tough talk was a little early. Though they had succeeded in pulling within three games of the Cubs, New York lost the final game of the series, and Chicago kept on winning after they left New York. A week later, the Mets did manage to take two out of three from the Cubs again—this time at Wrigley Field—but then they began a mini-slide, slipping to five and a half games back on July 15 and a full six games out by the end of the month. The Mets were back to treading water, and they needed to get very hot very quickly if they were going to make a run at the pennant.

National League East Standings: July 31, 1969

TEAM	W	L	PCT	GB
Chicago	64	41	.610	—
New York	**55**	**44**	**.556**	**6**
St. Louis	55	49	.529	8½
Pittsburgh	53	50	.515	10

In the middle of August, the Mets made their move. Seaver, who was 15-7 at the time, started a personal ten-game winning streak that would extend for the rest of the regular season. He emerged as the team's inspiration, leading by example and motivating his teammates to pull together and give 100% as a team.

The wins came left and right. From August 18th until the end of the month, the Mets won eleven and lost only two. Everyone pitched in. Shortstop Bud Harrelson (brother of Ken, the '67 Sox standout), had missed action early in the season because of military reserve duty and now returned to play flawless defense. Harrelson was certainly no slugger, but his hits were timely and valuable. Cleon Jones, playing left field and occasionally first base, was putting together a career year at the plate; he'd end the season with a .340 average, 12 homers, 75 RBIs, and 16 stolen bases in only 137 games. The righty/lefty platoon of Donn Clendenon and Ed Kranepool worked out nicely at first base; Wayne Garrett and Ed Charles performed capably at third as did Ken Boswell and Al Weis at second. Center fielder Tommie Agee, who had emerged as the team's only "regular" position player, provided good power and moderate speed: by season's end, he'd have 26 homers and 12 stolen bases.

With the team on a roll, members of the Mets suddenly found themselves inundated with visits from "old friends." Kranepool, the only holdover from the original 1962 Mets, told sportswriters, "This is what happens when you're winning. People call you for tickets. People drop by to say hello and offer congratulations. This hasn't happened in seven years. We've caught everybody by surprise. And, frankly, we weren't that sure of ourselves, either."

On September 3rd, the Cubs were shut out by the Cincinnati Reds. The loss initiated a mammoth slide; Chicago lost eight in a row and eleven of twelve. Two of these games—on September 8th and 9th—were at the hands of Jerry Koosman, Tom Seaver and company. Koosman beat them 3-2, while Seaver held them to five hits to win 7-1. When the dust settled, the surging Mets were a scant half game behind the ragged and demoralized Cubbies. There were 23 games left on the Mets' schedule.

The next day New York swept a doubleheader from the Montreal Expos, 3-2 and 7-1. Young Nolan Ryan gave a preview of things to come with his outstanding complete-game victory in the second game: he allowed only three hits while striking out eleven. Meanwhile, in Philadelphia, the Cubs had lost to the Phillies, 6-2. When the news was flashed on the scoreboard, Shea Stadium went into a frenzy. The New York Mets were all alone in first place.

At the end of the day there was a bottle or two of cheap champagne in the Mets clubhouse, but the players remained level-headed. A cool and composed Seaver told the press, "I think being in first place will just make us tougher and help us. We always did believe in ourselves, but each time you win the belief grows."

Gil Hodges added, "Our players are young but confident and, experienced or not so experienced, they've kept belief in themselves when things went badly for a while. I knew we'd have an improved team, but I didn't really anticipate we'd develop quite so quickly."

National League East Standings: September 11, 1969				
TEAM	W	L	PCT	GB
New York	**84**	**57**	**.596**	—
Chicago	84	59	.587	1
St. Louis	77	65	.542	7½
Pittsburgh	75	64	.540	8

It was happening. It was actually happening. The lowly Mets had a grip on first, and their surging legion of disciples was ecstatic. *New York Post* writer Pete Hamill wrote, "Don't talk to me today about Biafra or Nixon or Vietnam or John Lindsay. The Mets are leading the league. Get out of the way and sing us no more sad songs. I'm going drinking. It's September and the Mets are leading the league."

They would continue to lead, too. The Mets won ten in a row, 13 of 14, and 24 of their last 31. As the team surged toward the divisional title, the huge city it represented fell unashamedly in love with the "losers" who had turned everything around.

★   ★   ★

"They're going to win a pennant or something. That's nice."

— Truman Capote, September 1969

On September 20th, the first-place Mets were the victims of an embarrassing no-hitter by Pittsburgh Pirate hurler Bob Moose. But four days later, they beat the St. Louis Cardinals—the same Cardinals who were supposed to have run away with the flag—and clinched the divisional title. In that game, Gary Gentry tossed a five-hit, complete game shutout while Donn

Clendenon smashed two homers and Ed Charles added another. After the Mets turned a double play to end the game, the crowd spilled past security and onto the field. Shea Stadium was in chaos. It took some players twenty minutes to claw their way back to the clubhouse.

The Mets, the toast of New York, finished off the regular season in high style, winning nine of their last ten. Seaver ended up at 25-7 with a 2.21 ERA and was honored with the first of his three Cy Young Awards. The sorry Cubs, riddled with injuries and overworked by a panicking Leo Durocher, limped through the end of the season. Their stretch drive had been a joke: Chicago lost 18 of its final 26 games. The final standings could have fooled one into thinking there had been no pennant race at all.

Final 1969 National League East Standings

TEAM	W	L	PCT	GB
New York	100	62	.617	—
Chicago	92	70	.568	8
Pittsburgh	88	74	.543	12
St. Louis	87	75	.537	13
Philadelphia	63	99	.389	37
Montreal	52	110	.321	48

The Mets faced the National League West champion Atlanta Braves in the first National League Championship Series. With sluggers like Hank Aaron, Orlando Cepeda, and Rico Carty, the Braves were a powerful team. But Mets pitching held Atlanta bats in check—though Aaron did homer in each game—and the suddenly potent New York bats continued their torrid autumn clip. Tommie Agee and Ken Boswell each smashed two home runs in the series; Cleon Jones posted a .429 playoff average; outfielder Art Shamsky was even better at .538. The Mets swept the stunned Braves, three games to none. Tom Seaver, Nolan Ryan, and Ron Taylor each earned a win en route to the National League pennant.

★ ★ ★

Marcel Marceau is not supposed to talk. Linus is not supposed to lose his blanket. When you drop an apple, it's supposed to fall downward. The Mets were not supposed to play in the World Series.

But there it was in black and white. The Mets were facing the Baltimore Orioles, winners of 109 regular-season games, in baseball's 65th fall classic. "We're here to prove that there is no Santa Claus," intoned one media-weary Oriole.

The Series began on October 11th at Baltimore's Memorial Stadium with Seaver facing 23-game-winner Mike Cuellar. Things got off to a rocky start for the visitors when Baltimore's leadoff hitter, Don Buford, cracked Seaver's second pitch into the stands. Tom Terrific, the heart and soul of the team, gave up three more runs and left after the fifth inning. The Mets proved they were only human by suffering their first postseason defeat.

Behind the pitching of Koosman and Taylor, however, New York tied the Series the next day. Koosman allowed only two hits during the 2-1 squeaker. The victory was a shot in the arm, proof that New York could make a go of it in the biggest games. Hodges and his boys were heading back to New York with the World Series tied at one game apiece.

Back at Shea on October 14th, the Mets rocked Jim Palmer; Agee and Kranepool each homered. Agee was also something of a wizard in center field, making several diving catches to rob Oriole hitters of extra bases. Gary Gentry threw smoke for seven innings and, before yielding to reliever Nolan Ryan, smacked a two-run double himself. When it was over, the Mets had won, 5-0, to go up two games to one in the series.

Seaver took the mound in Game Four and fared much better than in his first outing. With the Mets leading 1-0, he held the Orioles scoreless until the ninth inning, when Ron Swoboda turned Brooks Robinson's seeming-extra-base hit into a sacrifice fly by making an amazing one-handed diving catch in right center field. Seaver got out of the inning; the contest was tied, 1-1, after nine. In the bottom of the tenth—with the score still tied—Jerry Grote doubled and Al Weis was intentionally walked. Second-string catcher J.C. Martin, called upon to pinch hit for Seaver, was ordered to bunt. Martin bunted back to the pitcher, who fielded the ball cleanly but hit Martin with his throw to first. The ball dribbled into the outfield and Grote scored the winning run. The Mets were one victory away from a world championship.

The Orioles jumped to a 3-0 lead early in Game Five, but the Mets came back in the sixth inning. Cleon Jones was hit on the foot with a Dave McNally curve—and he proved it to the umpire by pointing out the shoe-polish mark left on the ball. After Jones took his base, Donn Clendenon followed with a mammoth home run. Al Weis's solo homer tied it in the seventh, and the Mets scored twice more on errors and doubles in the eighth. Leading, 5-3, Koosman finished off the Orioles in the top of the ninth to cap the championship. It was over. Shea Stadium erupted for what seemed like the hundredth time in the past several weeks.

★　★　★

Baseball—and perhaps America—would never be the same. An expansion team—the *worst* expansion team ever—had won the World Series. Walking on the moon was one thing, but for the *Mets* to win the World Series . . .

In 1969, a baseball team from New York showed an increasingly cynical and polarized country that anything, really, is possible. Years after the Mets' miracle, former infielder Ed Charles said, "I'm sure, I'm positive, I know there were people who changed their lives because of the Miracle Mets. People felt better. It was a good thing." He was right.

CHAPTER EIGHT

A MADNESS TO THEIR METHOD

THE 1978 NEW YORK YANKEES

THE YEAR BEFORE

Final 1977 American League East Standings

TEAM	W	L	PCT	GB
New York	**100**	**62**	**.617**	—
Baltimore	97	64	.602	2½
Boston	97	64	.602	2½
Detroit	74	88	.457	26
Cleveland	71	90	.441	28½
Milwaukee	67	95	.414	33
Toronto	54	107	.335	45½

"October. That's when they pay off for playing ball."

— REGGIE JACKSON

Most of the teams profiled here were chosen because they had a great year after coming off a lousy one. In many cases, these longshot teams had a long history of mediocrity (or worse) before they beat the odds. The Yankees are the only team in this book that won the world championship the year before they were longshots. Admittedly, their case is a strange one that merits some explanation.

The Yankees tore apart the A.L. East in '77 with their bats, their gloves, their pitching, and their combative and controversial skipper Billy Martin. In a tough divisional race, they weathered strong finishes by the Baltimore Orioles and Boston Red Sox to take the divisional crown. They went on to stage one of the most dramatic come-from-behind victories in American League Championship Series history when they defeated the Kansas City Royals.

And, of course, it's hard to forget the '77 World Series, which pitted the Yanks against one of Tommy Lasorda's best L.A. Dodger lineups. Yankee right fielder Reggie Jackson's performance is still regarded as one of the finest in World Series history. He reminded the world why he was nicknamed "Mr. October" by hitting five home runs—three of them on the first pitch of three consecutive at-bats in the final game.

Even after such a stellar year, the Bronx Bombers found the odds stacked against them in 1978—but not for lack of talent. Their '78 starting lineup was essentially identical to that of the previous year. And with the exception of losing starter Mike Torrez to the Red Sox (a loss they countered by acquiring quality reliever Rich Gossage from the Pirates), the pitching staff was intact, too.

The seeds of Yankee discontent in 1978 lay in the myriad personal and professional distractions the team faced. Psychologically, it was not an easy year—even if it did culminate in a championship.

★ ★ ★

For the first half of the season, this was a club constantly teetering on the edge of a collective nervous breakdown. Nary a day passed in which a member of the Yankees—or club owner George Steinbrenner—failed to make headlines for something that happened off the field. Players, manager, and owner attacked each other relentlessly through the New York tabloid press. The team switched exclusively to chartered flights after one horrified civilian too many complained of drunken, raucous behavior on commercial flights. If the '62 Mets were lovable losers, the '78 Yankees seemed bent on proving themselves sociopathic title holders.

The man at the top was no help. Steinbrenner feuded constantly with his players and staff, most of whom loathed him. He also developed a habit of impulsively firing his managers; Ralph Houk and Bill Virdon lasted just a year apiece under the Steinbrenner regime. Billy Martin, hired in 1975, carried the team to the pennant the next year and the world championship the following season. Martin was still around as the 1978 season began. Before his death in late 1989, however, Martin would be fired and hired by George Steinbrenner five separate times.

Still, no one could get too haughty with Steinbrenner for his inability to get along with Martin, a notoriously difficult man to work with. The manager courted disaster. Billy Martin drank like a fish, not unusual for a big-league manager. What *was* unusual was that he simply could not steer clear of barroom brawls. The back pages of the New York tabloids were constantly relating some drunken fight or another the Yankee manager had gotten into. Usually, Martin would start them—allegedly under the pretense of "defending his team's honor." In their superb book *Damned Yankees*, authors Bill Madden and Moss Klein compiled the hilarious "Billy Martin Ring Record," which chronicles all of the documented brawls Martin participated in, dating back to 1952. (There were eighteen.) Sportswriter Jim Murray summed it up when he wrote, "Some people have a chip on their shoulder. Billy [Martin] has a whole lumberyard." With the pressure to repeat as world champions in 1978, Martin seemed more explosive than ever.

Originally, Martin hadn't thought he'd get a shot at being a manager. As a player at the tail end of his career in 1961, he had been asked about the prospects of becoming a big league skipper. "I don't think so," he replied, "I've got the reputation for being baseball's bad boy and I don't deserve it. But I think I'd make a good manager. For one thing, I know how to handle men. That's the secret of managing. For another, I know enough about the game, not fundamentals, but executing. I think I could get the most out of players with common sense and psychology. I'm fiery enough and I'd have their respect. Unfortunately, I don't think I'll ever get the chance and there's nothing in the world can change that."

Of course, Billy Martin got his chance to manage and proved to be an excellent—if, as advertised, fiery—skipper. He had a tougher time than he thought, however, when it came to "handling men"—especially a man named Jackson.

Reggie Jackson was, of course, an amazing clutch hitter who had been at the center of the Oakland A's dynasty of the early '70s. He got along with virtually no one in the Yankee organization, least of all Billy Martin. His admirers called him the most dynamic slugger in the American League. Critics called him a hypertalkative pseudo-intellectual with an over inflated ego. Indeed, Jackson had a penchant for aggravating other Yankees—and especially Billy Martin—by making inflammatory statements to the press. When the Yankees signed him as a free agent in 1976, Jackson got off on the wrong foot by snubbing manager Martin. At the press conference after the signing, Jackson didn't mention his new manager's name, saying only, "I'm very happy to be coming to the Yankees to play for George Steinbrenner." From that point on, Martin and Jackson played Hatfields-and-McCoys in one of baseball's most notorious feuds.

That Jackson had a big head was not likely to be disputed, even by Yankee partisans. The Reggie Bar—the first candy bar to be named after a ballplayer since the Oh Henry! honored Hank Aaron in the early 1970s—was unveiled late in the 1977 season. It did absolutely nothing to control Jackson's mammoth ego, and it probably didn't help his shaky fielding, either. Once, team punster Graig Nettles cracked, "What does he need another candy bar for? He's already got one—Butterfingers." Jackson refused to speak to him for weeks.

At one point, when Reggie Bars were being given out to Yankee Stadium patrons as a promotion, Jackson was mired in one of his worst slumps and striking out more often than usual. (This is saying something—he struck out swinging all too often and eventually went on to become the all-time strikeout king.) Thousands of Reggie Bars showered onto the field when he came to the plate. After a tough at-bat, Jackson would sometimes be pelted with the candy bars while roaming right field. His teammates (and, presumably, Bill Martin) loved it. But Yankee management quickly halted the free Reggie Bar promotions.

There were other Yankee personalities. Mickey Rivers, the swift of foot and slick of glove center fielder, was a lovable character—but a headache to manage. Full of potential, Rivers had an aggravating habit of giving a hundred percent only when it suited him. He was quick and streetwise, but he loved to play dumb. His most widely quoted aphorism was actually quite profound, and may reflect how he got through 1978: "Ain't no sense in worrying about things you got control over, 'cause if you got control over them, ain't no sense worrying. And there ain't no sense worrying about things you got no control over, 'cause if you got no control over them, ain't no sense worrying about them."

By 1978, Rivers had become well known for his enthusiasm for betting on horses. Many a post-game evening was spent by Mick the Quick and a teammate or two at the local track. Usually, he lost. When he did win, he'd "reinvest" his winnings. Eventually, he requested salary advances to support his betting. On more than one occasion, he was denied an advance and reacted with lazy play in the field. This did little to enhance team unity on a team that needed it desperately.

★ ★ ★

In 1977—although they finished 2½ games behind the Yankees—the Boston Red Sox displayed almost unbelievable power. Jim Rice blossomed as a slugger and hit 39 round-trippers. Veteran Carl Yastrzemski had 28, George "Boomer" Scott had 33, and catcher Carlton Fisk had 26. Even the number nine hitter, third baseman Butch Hobson, belted 30 homers. During one stretch, the Red Sox swatted thirty-three home runs in the course of just ten games.

After the '77 season ended, Sox management was not content to simply stay with the fence-busting roster that brought them a 97-64 record that year. They solidified their pitching staff by acquiring righthanders Dennis Eckersley (from the Indians) and Mike Torrez (snatched from the Yankees after his heroics in the 1977 postseason). Then they promoted a smokeballing relief specialist named Bob Stanley from the minors. Finally, speedy second baseman Jerry Remy was picked up from the Angels to replace Denny Doyle, a mediocre veteran.

With the team now healthy, enthusiastic, and working harmoniously, the Boston Red Sox were poised to dominate baseball in 1978. They were favored to take the division. The Yankees, it was assumed, had too many personality clashes and management conflicts to be a real winner. Surely, the thinking went, they would self-destruct somewhere between April and September. As the Yankee season unfolded, the prognosticators looked pretty good.

And baseball soothsayers were right about the Red Sox, too—at least for the first half of the season. Early on, Boston was nearly unbeatable. Jim Rice was blasting home runs at a rate that would break Roger Maris's home run record, and the team was on a pace to eclipse the Indians' record of 111 regular-season wins.

On May 16th, Billy Martin celebrated his 50th birthday. His office at Yankee Stadium was adorned with a new plaque that read, "EXTRAORDINARY ACHIEVEMENT AWARD TO BILLY MARTIN, FOR HAVING REACHED THE AGE OF FIFTY WITHOUT BEING MURDERED BY SOMEONE . . . TO THE AMAZEMENT OF ALL WHO KNOW HIM." Even Billy got a chuckle from the gag, but there was more truth to it than anyone would let on.

The Yanks were battling the Brewers and Orioles for a shot at second place. Second-year lefty Ron "Louisiana Lightning" Guidry was creating a stir by winning his first 13 games. He would go on to post the best season for a starting pitcher in modern baseball. Even this early in the season, Guidry was being weighed against Jim Rice as an MVP candidate.

Despite Ron Guidry's outstanding performance, the Yankees were still considered hopeless. By mid-season, they were light-years behind the Red Sox, the victims of countless feuds, squabbles, and injuries. Hardnosed team leader Thurman Munson's injuries prevented him from doing much catching. He spent time in the outfield and at DH and was experiencing a severe power drop-off. Munson's type of injuries—not severe enough to warrant a placement on the disabled list, but bad enough to affect performance—were cropping up all over the Yankee roster; Mickey Rivers, Willie Randolph, and Bucky Dent each were hurt and playing poorly.

If the hitters had a few nagging injuries holding them back, the pitching staff was a triage unit. Jim "Catfish" Hunter suffered an offseason accident that apparently triggered diabetes. His arm was in constant pain; he was told he might never pitch again. Andy Messersmith, Dick Tidrow, and Ed Figueroa all missed starts because of sore arms. Minor leaguers were shuttled to and from New Haven for big league auditions. The pitching situation was so bad that on several occasions first baseman Jim Spencer warmed up in the bullpen for a possible stint on the mound.

By July 20th, the Yankees had fallen to fourth place. The team was written off by the New York press as finished for the year.

American League East Standings: July 20, 1978

TEAM	W	L	PCT	GB
Boston	62	28	.689	—
Milwaukee	53	37	.589	9
Baltimore	51	42	.548	12½
New York	**49**	**42**	**.538**	**13½**

On July 23, Billy Martin finally reached the breaking point. The manager was approached by a couple of reporters at O'Hare Airport after a game at Comiskey Park and was asked about his mounting problems with Reggie Jackson and George Steinbrenner. The frazzled manager was deadly serious when he said, "One's a born liar and the other's convicted." (The conviction he referred to resulted when Steinbrenner made illegal campaign contributions to Richard Nixon's reelection efforts in 1972.)

Martin's quote hit the New York papers the next day with the force of a hydrogen bomb. An enraged Steinbrenner immediately demanded his resignation and replaced him with Bob Lemon, the former Cleveland Indians pitching star and ex-manager of the White Sox.

Five days after Martin's departure, during an Old-Timers' game at Yankee Stadium, it was announced over the PA system that Bob Lemon would return as Yankee manager in 1979. It was strange to state this publicly so early in a new manager's tenure. Furthermore, an Old-Timers' game hardly seemed the appropriate atmosphere to divulge such an important piece of official news. Something was afoot.

A minute later, the speakers rang out with the news that none other than Billy Martin would be back as manager in 1980. The astonished crowd broke into a chorus of cheers that turned into a ten-minute standing ovation when Billy himself trotted out onto the field—wearing his Yankee pinstripes, no less. The New York sports media, with no pennant race to cover, ate it up.

While New York was being turned inside out with the George and Billy Show, the Red Sox were in the midst of a horrendous road trip. At one point, they lost nine of ten. But who was worrying in Boston? The lead was still intact.

American League East Standings: August 2, 1978

TEAM	W	L	PCT	GB
Boston	64	39	.625	—
Milwaukee	59	42	.584	4½
New York	**59**	**46**	**.562**	**6½**
Baltimore	57	46	.553	7½

Like Billy Martin, Bob Lemon liked to knock back a few drinks. Supposedly, he once said, "I drink after wins, I drink after losses, and I drink after rain outs." The two managers' similarities ended there, however. While Martin focused on offensive tactics, Lemon—himself a Hall of Fame pitcher—concentrated on his pitching staff. Martin was high-strung and unpredictable whereas Lemon was easy-going and rational. For Martin, baseball was a life-or-death affair. Lemon once stated that "baseball is a kid's game that grownups only tend to screw up."

Under Lemon, pitching suddenly found a groove. While Ron Guidry continued his superhuman pace and reliever Rich Gossage marched toward a Fireman of the Year award, Ed Figueroa came out of the woodwork and started piling up wins. Catfish Hunter returned after surgery and found he could pitch like a twenty-year-old again. Around the middle of August, the Yankees won ten of twelve games. But the Red Sox rebounded from their road woes and started to win again, and the Yanks couldn't gain much ground. Lemon just kept smiling and told his crew to "go have some fun."

★　★　★

On August 10th, the major New York newspapers went on strike. With just a handful of reporters from suburban papers traveling with and covering the team, Bob Lemon and the Yankees caught a break. Suddenly, media relations—which had always been a nightmare with Billy Martin at the helm—were nothing to worry about. The team could finally concentrate on baseball rather than newspaper-fueled feuds and other off-field fiascos.

After the season, Lemon commented, "I hated to see the newspaper guys out of work, but the strike, coming when it did, did more for us than if we picked up a twenty-game winner . . . Without those back pages screaming about stuff every day, I was able to keep things quieter."

The strike would continue for the rest of the regular season. The pressure-cooker atmosphere was gone.

American League East Standings: August 30, 1978

TEAM	W	L	PCT	GB
Boston	83	47	.638	—
New York	**75**	**54**	**.581**	**7½**
Milwaukee	75	56	.573	8½
Detroit	73	58	.557	10½

Around this time, sportswriter Chip Ainsworth was covering baseball for the *Valley Advocate* when he ventured into the Yankee clubhouse during a rain delay at Fenway Park. He related the following story:

The Yankees were all crowded around a small TV watching the past week's fielding highlights around the majors. Graig Nettles was shown making diving play after diving play at the hot corner. He was quietly having a great year in the field and appeared on this highlight program far more than any other player.

The rain continued outside. A Fenway food service worker entered the room with a huge bowl full of tiny, bite-sized Reggie Bars. It seems the manufacturers of the confection were trying out a different, promotional size. Nettles saw the bowl of Reggie Bars and jumped on the chance to draw attention away from his great plays. He stood in front of the screen, blocking everyone's view and held a mini Reggie Bar in each hand above his head. Then he proclaimed, "Hey, check these out. Now they make 'em little so the little kids can throw 'em, too!" The clubhouse erupted in laughter.

Now not even teammate-taunting, it seemed, could wreck the Bombers' groove. The Yankees were cruising, playing like a well-oiled machine. They went on a tear, winning 14 of 15 games during one stretch.

Meanwhile, the Red Sox were crumbling. After enjoying an almost totally healthy first half of the season, it was Boston's turn to deal with a wave of injuries: Fred Lynn and Carlton Fisk were worn out, Carl Yastrzemski had back and wrist problems, Dwight Evans was beaned and suffered from dizzy spells, Rick Burleson had a bad ankle, Jerry Remy wrenched his wrist, and Butch Hobson had bone chips floating in his elbow. Boston manager Don Zimmer didn't help matters by playing these regulars—injured or not—into the ground. The lead that had looked insurmountable was dwindling. The Yankees were moving within striking distance. People in Boston got a strange, terrified look in their eyes.

American League East Standings: September 4, 1978				
TEAM	W	L	PCT	GB
Boston	85	50	.630	—
New York	**79**	**55**	**.590**	**5½**
Milwaukee	78	58	.574	7½
Baltimore	76	61	.555	10

On September 7th, with the Yankees only four games behind the Red Sox, the two teams met in Fenway Park for a make-or-break four-game showdown. New York fans had high hopes: perhaps their team could take three out of four from the slumping Sox. No one was bold enough to predict the carnage that followed.

The series became known as the "Boston Massacre." During the course of the four games, not a single Red Sox starter made it out of the fourth inning. Boston defense took on a Little League quality, accounting for 12 errors. For four games the Yankees shelled the Red Sox mercilessly, spraying 67 hits, scoring 42 runs while giving up just 9, batting .396 as a team, and sweeping the series.

To add insult to injury, during the final game of the Boston humiliation, longtime Red Sox PA announcer Sherm Feller was conked between the eyes by a Thurman Munson foul ball. Feller was okay; the Red Sox were not. Their undisputed five-month domination of the A.L. East was over; New York and Boston were in a dead heat for first place. It was now a 20-game season.

After the fourth game, an anonymous Yankee told reporters matter-of-factly, "If Billy Martin were still here, we wouldn't be." Nobody disagreed. With a little help from the newspaper strikes, the easy-going Lemon had quietly turned his troubled team around 180 degrees. There was no more back-stabbing, no dissension, no brawls. Players concerned themselves with winning baseball games. "This is the way I like it," a contented Lemon was to say. "You guys play, and I sit in the dugout and enjoy."

American League East Standings: September 11, 1978

TEAM	W	L	PCT	GB
Boston	86	56	.606	—
New York	**86**	**56**	**.606**	—
Milwaukee	82	61	.573	4½
Baltimore	80	62	.563	6

The Yankees kept on soaring while the Red Sox continued to spiral downwards.

By September 17th, the Yankees held a 3½-game lead over Boston. But the season took one more twist. The Yankees won a few and lost a few, while the Red Sox regained their composure and went on a tear, winning 11 of 13. With one game left in the regular season, the Sox had scratched back to just a single game behind the Yankees. If the Sox were going down, it would not be without a struggle.

The baseball world held its breath on October 1st, the final day of the regular season. The Yankees had to beat the Cleveland Indians, *or* the Red Sox had to lose to the expansion Toronto Blue Jays; either result would clinch the division title for New York. A Yankee loss coupled with a Red Sox win, however, would tie the two teams and force a divisional playoff for the right to face the Kansas City Royals, who had long ago sewn up the A.L. West title.

Red Sox hurler Luis Tiant tossed a 2-hitter against the weak Blue Jays to win 5-0. An erratic Catfish Hunter gave up five earned runs in $1\frac{1}{3}$ innings, and the Yankees wound up losing to the lowly Indians, 9-2.

After a rollercoaster season, the Yankees and Red Sox ended the year with identical records. There would be a one-game playoff on October 2nd.

American League East Standings: October 2, 1978

TEAM	W	L	PCT	GB
New York	**99**	**63**	**.611**	—
Boston	99	63	.611	—
Milwaukee	93	69	.574	6½
Baltimore	90	71	.559	9

Boston won the coin toss and received the home field advantage. Don Zimmer started Mike Torrez against his former teammates. The ex-Yankee had been a pitching hero in the previous year's World Series; he signed a big-money contract with the Red Sox upon becoming a free agent. Surprising no one, Lemon started his ace, Ron Guidry, now the owner of a staggering 24-3 record.

Carl Yastrzemski, who had been baffled by Guidry's pitching throughout the season, lined a homer off the Louisiana lefty in the second inning to put the Sox on the board first. Yaz, nearing retirement, later admitted that he viewed this game as his last shot at acquiring a world championship ring.

The Red Sox made it 2-0 in the sixth when Jim Rice singled a run in. Red Sox fans could be forgiven for remaining uneasy; suffering under a 60-year world championship drought, they would have been nervous with a 15-run lead in the ninth. ("What a shame it would be to win 196 games in two years and not win anything," a contemplative Don Zimmer had said before the game.)

The Sox had a chance to add to the lead when Fred Lynn came up with two on and two out in the bottom of the sixth. The left-handed Lynn was not known for pulling the ball, especially against lefties, but Yankee right fielder Lou Piniella, for reasons even he could never explain, decided to shift towards the foul line—almost twenty yards away from where he normally played Lynn. Guidry delivered and Lynn pulled a scorching line drive down the right field line. Piniella was there, however; he gloved the ball easily and robbed Lynn of a sure two-run double that could have broken the game wide open for the Sox. The score remained 2-0, Boston.

In the top of the seventh, Torrez got Graig Nettles to fly out, then gave up back-to-back singles to Chris Chambliss and Roy White. Pinch hitter Jim Spencer flied out. Up stepped Bucky Dent.

The Yankees' scrappy shortstop was hitting all of .243 on the year and was never considered a power threat—having managed just 22 home runs in over 2,600 lifetime at-bats. As he settled into the batter's box, the wind shifted and started blowing out to left field. Dent fouled Torrez' second pitch off his foot. As he jumped around in pain, the ever-observant Mickey Rivers—who was on deck—noticed that his teammate's bat had a slight crack. Rivers ran into the dugout to get a new one for Dent, who later said he probably wouldn't have noticed the crack.

Dent stepped back into the box with his new piece of wood and took a chop at Torrez' first offering. All of New England breathed a collective sigh of relief at what appeared to be a high pop-up to left. Yastrzemski moved back to the warning track. Years later, the left fielder wrote of the moment in his autobiography, *Yaz*: "I could have expected it to come down to me on the warning track . . . except on that fall day, because [Dent] had gotten it so high, because the wind had shifted . . . Even when I got to the warning track I expected it to come down. Then I expected it to hit the Wall. I was shocked when it didn't. It landed in the screen. A three run homer for Bucky Dent." The Yankees had jumped ahead, 3-2.

A shaken Torrez proceeded to walk Rivers before yielding to reliever Bob Stanley. Thurman Munson came to bat and promptly rocked a Stanley pitch for an RBI double. Stanley settled down and retired the side. The Yanks led, 4-2. Rich Gossage came in and retired the Red Sox in the bottom of the seventh.

Reggie Jackson, as though suddenly remembering what month it was, led off the top of the eighth with a towering home run to dead center to pad the Yankee lead to three runs. Gossage lost a bit of his stuff in the bottom of the eighth, however, giving up a leadoff double to Jerry Remy and an RBI single to Yaz. That made it 5-3, Yankees. With one out, Carlton

Fisk singled and Fred Lynn followed by knocking Yaz home with another single. The Red Sox were only one run down. Billy Martin surely would have yanked the floundering Gossage by now. But Bob Lemon knew better. After a conference on the mound, Goose bore down and got the final two outs of the eighth.

The Yankees failed to score in their half of the ninth, so it went to the bottom of the ninth inning with the score 5-4, New York. With one out, Gossage gave up a walk to Rick Burleson. Jerry Remy followed with a hard line drive to right field. Piniella lost the ball in the setting sun, but nevertheless pounded his glove as though he had a bead on it. The decoy worked. Burleson held up between first and second, waiting for the ball to either fall in or be caught. It dropped for a single, but Burleson only got to second. Jim Rice followed with a long fly ball to center and Burleson advanced to third—rather than home. New England groaned. For the second time that day, Lou Piniella had burned the Red Sox in right field.

There were now two outs. Gossage had one last hurdle to clear: Carl Yastrzemski, who was 2-for-4 with a home run on the day.

The heart and soul of the star-crossed 1967 Sox, the undisputed heir to Teddy Ballgame, the man who, more than anyone else, seemed to have a right to retire with a championship under his belt, popped up to Graig Nettles in foul territory on the second pitch. Fenway Park resonated with a strange mixture of moans and cheers; about a third of the crowd had come up from New York.

One of the most grueling regular seasons ever was over, and the Yankees were ecstatic. Graig Nettles told baseball writer Thomas Boswell that he knew the Yankees would win the playoff game all along. "All I could think of," he said, "was Bobby Thomson and that '51 playoff. I figured if anybody was going to beat us, *those* were the guys."

A few years later, the result of a massive baseball fan survey would deem the '78 playoff contest the greatest game of the 1970s. Many baseball fans argue that Dent won the divisional title with his clutch bloop homer. Others point out that Jackson's home run provided the winning margin. Still others say that Piniella's wizardly work in right field kept at least three Boston runs from scoring. But in the end, the pertinent fact was that the Yankees had won. They had done so in the most unpredictable way imaginable: as a team.

Final 1978 American League East Standings

TEAM	W	L	PCT	GB
New York	100	63	.613	—
Boston	99	64	.607	1
Milwaukee	93	69	.574	6½
Baltimore	90	71	.559	9
Detroit	86	76	.531	13½
Cleveland	69	90	.434	29
Toronto	59	102	.366	40

The Yankees had little time to celebrate their divisional title. They took a plane from Boston to Kansas City, where the Royals met them in the American League playoffs for the third straight year.

Despite George Brett's three home runs in Game 3 and .389 series average, the Royals could only pull off one victory (in Game 2) against the adrenaline-fueled Yankees. Reggie Jackson continued his annual October assault on pitchers, leading Yankee hitters with a .462 playoff average and two homers. On October 7th, with his team ahead two games to one, Ron Guidry hurled a brilliant Game 4, allowing only one Royal run and wrapping up the American League pennant. In 1976 and 1977, the Yankees—under Billy Martin—had to work for the pennant. In each of those playoffs, the Yankees edged out the Royals, three games to two. This year they had an easier time of it. It was as though beating the Red Sox had made other contests, even the American League Championship Series, trivial.

The Dodgers, who had just beaten the Phillies for the National League pennant, were out for revenge. Lasorda and company were still smarting from the previous year's Yankee mauling. Furthermore, former Dodger infielder and longtime coach Jim Gilliam had just died of a brain hemorrhage two days before the Series began; the team was out to win it all for a fallen friend.

In Los Angeles for the first two games, the Dodgers played their hearts out. In Game 1 they shellacked the Yankees, 11-5; four Yankee pitchers—Ed Figueroa, Ken Clay, Paul Lindblad, and Dick Tidrow—gave up a total of 15 hits. The next evening, Burt Hooten floated his baffling knuckleball past Yankee hitters for six-plus innings, giving up three runs.

The Dodger bullpen took over in the seventh and shut the Yanks out for the remainder of the game. Catfish Hunter, meanwhile, continued to have trouble. In six innings, he surrendered four runs—enough to lose the game, 4-3, and put the Yankees down in the Series, two games to none.

After a travel day, the Series moved to New York, where Yankee fans awaited their heroes. Ron Guidry was rested enough to make a bid at turning things around. Guidry was in fine form, tossing a complete game, striking out four and allowing just one run. After the 5-1 Yankee win, Guidry was the first to admit he owed Graig Nettles a tip of the hat. The third baseman had made four diving plays of Brooks Robinson vintage to save at least three and possibly four Dodger runs.

In Game 4, the Yankees trailed 3-0 in the fifth inning, but came back to tie it in the eighth. In the tenth inning, Roy White walked, Reggie Jackson singled, and Lou Piniella knocked in the winning run off Dodger reliever Bob Welch. The Series was tied up at two games apiece.

Game 5 was a breeze for the Yanks. They exploded for 12 runs on 18 hits and set a World Series record by hitting 16 singles in one game. The Dodgers committed three errors and couldn't touch rookie pitcher Jim Beattie. After inducing Bill Russell to ground back to him, the youngster had gone all nine innings, striking out five and allowing just two runs. The Yanks won, 12-2. It was the first complete game of Beattie's major league career.

The Yankees were one win from capping the most improbable New York championship ever. Back in Los Angeles for Game 6, Catfish Hunter got back into his comeback mode. He and Goose Gossage combined to hold the Dodgers to two runs. As in the divisional playoff game two weeks earlier, the most unlikely bat in the lineup came alive: Bucky Dent went 3-for-4 with 3 RBIs on his way to capturing the Series MVP award. No-name second baseman Brian Doyle also chipped in, going 3-for-4 and knocking in two. And, of course, it wouldn't have been a World Series if Reggie hadn't contributed his two cents. In the seventh inning, Jackson launched a two-run blast into the center field bleachers. The Yankees won the game, 7-2, and the Series.

It was the first time a team had taken a world championship by winning four in a row after losing the first two. The strange pattern mirrored the remarkable regular season New York had recently completed: seeming collapse, reorganization, sudden invincibility. Even the Boss, George Steinbrenner, had to smile.

CHAPTER NINE

WORST TO FIRST TIMES TWO

THE ATLANTA BRAVES AND MINNESOTA TWINS OF 1991

THE YEAR BEFORE . . .

Final 1990 Standings: American League West

TEAM	W	L	PCT	GB
Oakland	103	59	.636	—
Chicago	94	68	.580	9
Texas	83	79	.512	20
California	80	82	.494	23
Seattle	77	85	.475	26
Kansas City	75	86	.466	27½
Minnesota	**74**	**88**	**.457**	**29**

Final 1990 Standings: National League West

TEAM	W	L	PCT	GB
Cincinnati	91	71	.562	—
Los Angeles	86	76	.531	5
San Francisco	85	77	.525	6
Houston	75	87	.463	16
San Diego	75	87	.463	16
Atlanta	**65**	**97**	**.401**	**26**

"Jack's an animal."

— TWINS THIRD BASEMAN MIKE PAGLIARULO,
ON TEAMMATE JACK MORRIS

The Minnesota Twins and Atlanta Braves were each coming off abysmal last-place finishes as the spring of 1991 rolled around. Baseball insiders and Las Vegas oddsmakers had written each club off almost without a thought.

In analyzing the Braves, widely picked to finish at the bottom of the barrel again, one preseason scribe wrote of youthful pitchers who were "unlikely to be more than adequate" and of a team "trying to get respectable while rebuilding." The experts were even harsher in their assessment of the Minnesota Twins. "There is little to suggest," *Baseball Digest* intoned wearily, "[that] the Twins, with their power waning, will rise again in 1991. Last place is likely."

★　★　★

The Braves had been in decline for quite some time. After winning the divisional title in 1982 and finishing in the running for the next couple of years, the club spent the rest of the 1980s and the 1990 season in last or second-to-last place. Ex-slugger Darrel Evans was nearing retirement, the infield was questionable, and the pitching staff was a mixture of road-weary journeymen and unproven youngsters.

The trade of outfielder Dale Murphy to the Philadelphia Phillies in mid-1990 was the last straw as far as Braves fans were concerned. Attendance at Fulton County Stadium plummeted to barely 5,000 per game. Televised Braves games, which were broadcast across the country on team owner Ted Turner's cable network, became a national joke; viewers only tuned in to catch the Braves' opponents.

Meanwhile, in Minneapolis, Twins fans still had the taste of the 1987 World Championship to savor, but somehow lacked confidence in their club. There was good reason for this—even beyond the team's last-place finish in 1990. Before the 1987 season, the state of Minnesota suffered from what seemed to many to be a professional sports "curse." It all started when the early Lakers fled to play basketball in Los Angeles. After they moved, they became the dominant force in the NBA.

The franchises that stayed in Minnesota appeared doomed. The North Stars had always put together a strong hockey team, but the only two times the Stars made it to the Stanley Cup finals, they lost. Likewise, the Vikings played in four Super Bowls—and lost every one of them.

The Twins seemed to suffer most of all. The club—originally called the Senators—moved from Washington to Minneapolis after the 1961 season, and for the most part was able to put contending squads on the field. But until 1987, they had a history strikingly similar to the Boston Red Sox in that they would come close to winning it all, drive their fans wild with anticipation, and fall short at the last minute. They had extremely close calls in 1965 (when they won the pennant), 1967, 1969, and 1970, and they usually finished over .500 in the 1970s. But they could never seem to cover the final ten yards.

To the casual observer, the Minnesota "curse" appeared finally to be lifted in the autumn of 1987 when the Twins came from behind to beat the St. Louis Cardinals in a dramatic World Series. Detractors, however, viewed the Series victory as an aberration. They cited as an excuse the fact that the home team won each game—and argued that the championship was actually decided by the Twins' four home dates and the glare of the Hubert H. Humphrey Metrodome ceiling. Another supposed blemish on the '87 Twins was their lackluster 85-77 regular season record. Minnesota's .525 winning percentage was the poorest by a World Series champion in baseball history.

It wasn't that the Twins were unloved; they became the first A.L. team to draw over three million spectators in one season. Their fans simply didn't trust them. Lifelong Twins fan Paul Hyde summed up popular sentiments when he said, "After the [1987] Series, sure, I was excited and joyful and goin' crazy and all that. But the truth is, I always believed they would fail. When they didn't fail, I was sure it was a fluke."

★   ★   ★

In March of 1991, John Coyle, a young businessman from Texas, was transferred by his company to Atlanta. A true sports nut, John always loved to root for the underdog; he looked forward to adopting the sorry Braves as his new team. With spring training in full swing, the new Atlanta resident—and freshly-converted Braves fan—studied and memorized the roster in anticipation of a losing—but fun—season.

One of Coyle's roommates, who had grown weary of following the pathetic club, decided to unload his pair of season tickets to the only person he knew would appreciate them. After all, with barely perceptible local interest in the team, the season tickets were not exactly a hot commodity. (At the time, one Atlanta resident explained that "attending a Braves game is nothing more than an excuse to leave work early.") The roommate gave the home-plate tickets to Coyle free of charge, having no idea they would soon be quite literally worth their weight in gold.

★　★　★

Braves manager Bobby Cox, like his 1914 counterpart George Stallings, was modest in his goals for the Braves. He vowed to do the best he could with the men available, and had no qualms about platooning and making frequent pitching changes. The skipper's deft handling of free agent acquisitions Terry Pendleton at third base and Rafael Belliard at shortstop was helping to solidify the team's defense—and adding some punch at the plate. It didn't hurt, either, that young lefthanders Steve Avery and Tom Glavine both got off to strong starts.

In the first half of the season, the Braves won a good deal more than they were expected to. By the All-Star break, they weren't exactly contending, but they had at least come a long way from their last-place 1990 performance. Midway through the season, the consensus in baseball circles was that the Braves were a pleasant surprise, a "feel-good" team that might develop into a contender in the coming years.

National League West Standings: 1991 All-Star break

TEAM	W	L	PCT	GB
Los Angeles	49	31	.613	—
Cincinnati	44	36	.550	5
Atlanta	**39**	**40**	**.494**	**9½**
San Diego	40	43	.482	10½

After the All-Star break, the Braves caught fire. They won 22 of 33 games to creep within striking distance of the Los Angeles Dodgers. One of their veterans, outfielder Lonnie Smith, who was supposedly washed up at age 35, started smacking the ball. Terry Pendleton, on his way to the National League MVP award, followed suit. The pitching staff—both the starting rotation and the bullpen—was establishing itself as the finest in the National League. Atlanta residents began to stare in disbelief at their morning papers, which seemed to indicate that the Braves had somehow become the hottest team in the league.

National League West Standings: August 15, 1991

TEAM	W	L	PCT	GB
Los Angeles	63	50	.558	—
Atlanta	**61**	**51**	**.545**	**1½**
San Francisco	56	57	.496	7
San Diego	56	58	.491	7½

Suddenly cable television subscribers across the country had a reason to tune in to Turner Network Television: there was a pennant race on. The stadium filled up. John Coyle's roommate kicked himself.

By now, Braves fever had taken the country by storm and baseball fans everywhere seemed to be doing the "tomahawk chop"—a chopping motion originated by Fulton County Stadium attendees in tribute to their rejuvenated Braves.

Atlanta merchants cashed in. Braves paraphernalia was everywhere. Department stores, airport shops, convenience stores, and sporting goods outlets all capitalized on the unexpected phenomenon. Businesses adjusted their work hours and morning traffic jams shifted from 7:30 to 10 o'clock. It had now become every Atlanta resident's duty to watch each game to the end, even if that meant a late start the next morning.

The Braves had gone from rags to riches in just a few short months. They had caught the Dodgers, but they would remain neck-and-neck with them into the final days of the season.

National League West Standings: September 1, 1991				
TEAM	W	L	PCT	GB
Atlanta	**72**	**57**	**.558**	—
Los Angeles	71	58	.550	1
Cincinnati	64	65	.496	8
San Diego	63	67	.485	9½

By this time, attending a Braves game was a luxury reserved for the lucky, the famous, and the powerful. Former President Jimmy Carter frequented games. Team owner Ted Turner and Jane Fonda—neither of whom, it seemed, had been sighted inside Fulton County Stadium in eons—were now conspicuously situated in the front row of virtually every game, cheering and chopping for their new Miracle Braves.

Although several wistful fans of baseball history reported seeing the ghosts of *Boston* Braves Rabbit Maranville, Bill James, and Hank Gowdy smiling in the bleachers, these appearances remain unconfirmed.

★ ★ ★

Like the Braves, the supposedly cursed Minnesota Twins got out of the starting gate in 1991 with greater speed than expected. Like the Braves, they showed no early signs of contending. By June 1st, the team was two games below .500 and in fifth place.

Many key Minnesota players from the 1987 championship team were no longer on board: Jeff Reardon, Frank Viola, Bert Blyleven, Gary Gaetti, and Tom Brunansky were all gone. Only two stars remained from the '87 World Series squad: sluggers Kent Hrbek and Kirby Puckett. Hrbek was having a solid year, but it was Puckett who had emerged as the heart and soul of the team. By mid-season, he was carrying the team with his .300-plus bat, superb defensive skills, likable leadership qualities, and unselfish play.

Twins manager Tom Kelly was hoping his pitching corps, which consisted of veteran Jack Morris and a bank of "no-names," would hit a groove to bring them into contention. In June, it happened. The Twins strung together an amazing 15-game win streak behind the strong arms of Morris, Scott Erickson, Mark Guthrie, and Kevin Tapani. Minnesota batters, struggling for power in recent years, averaged one home run per game during the fifteen games. The streak catapulted the Twins into the pennant race.

Unlike the Braves, the Twins found themselves in a virtual first-place tie at the All-Star break. Minnesota fans pricked up their ears and hoped for the best, but they couldn't help expecting the worst.

American League West Standings: 1991 All-Star break

TEAM	W	L	PCT	GB
Texas	44	33	.571	—
Minnesota	**47**	**36**	**.566**	—
California	44	37	.543	2
Chicago	43	37	.538	2½

The winningest pitcher of the 1980s, righthander Jack Morris had been acquired by the Twins from the Detroit Tigers in the offseason in the hopes of bringing some maturity to the team and perhaps taking some pressure off the bullpen. He had posted mediocre numbers for Detroit in 1990 (15-18, with a 4.51 ERA), but the 36-year-old won a spot in the starting rotation and soon regained his 1980s form. Morris's surly demeanor and tough-guy reputation put off some of his new teammates at first, but they soon came to realize that the new guy was simply a first-class competitor.

Morris, well known for his desire to complete games, once left Twins manager Tom Kelly speechless during spring training in 1991. "You're the manager," he said. "If you have to take me out of a game, do it. But don't expect me to like it." Morris backed up his talk; he proved to be virtually unstoppable in late-inning, high pressure situations.

By mid-August, the Twins had nabbed sole possession of first place and showed no signs of slowing down.

American League West Standings: August 15, 1991

TEAM	W	L	PCT	GB
Minnesota	**68**	**47**	**.591**	—
Chicago	66	48	.579	1½
Oakland	64	51	.557	4
Kansas City	60	52	.536	6½

As the season wore on, the Twins—bolstered by some key victories over the 1990 division champion Oakland A's—started to pull away from the pack. By September, the injury-riddled A's and the floundering Chicago White Sox wallowed far behind, well out of striking distance.

Suddenly the Twins were making things look easy.

American League West Standings: September 1, 1991

TEAM	W	L	PCT	GB
Minnesota	**78**	**53**	**.595**	—
Oakland	71	60	.542	7
Chicago	69	61	.531	8½
Kansas City	67	61	.523	9½
Texas	67	61	.523	9½

None of the other American League West teams could mount a comeback. The Twins coasted easily through September to the divisional title.

It was the comeback players who contributed the most to the Twins' surprising season. Third baseman Mike Pagliarulo ended the year at .279—40 points above his career average. Jack Morris, of course, returned to his classic form. Perennial substitute outfielder Shane Mack hit .310 on the year, having finally nailed down an everyday job. Veteran designated hitter Chili Davis provided much of the club's power, cracking 29 homers and 93 RBIs. Brian Harper emerged as baseball's best-hitting catcher, batting .311—an unusually high average for a backstop.

With the regular season wrapped up, the Twins now looked ahead to facing the Toronto Blue Jays in the American League playoffs.

Interestingly, for the first time in the history of divisional play, the two teams competing in the playoffs ended the regular season with a three-game series against each other. Although, with both divisional races decided, the results of those three games were meaningless, both the Twins and the Blue Jays took advantage of the series and made last-minute efforts to size up the opposition. (The Blue Jays took the series, two games to one.)

Final 1991 American League West Standings

TEAM	W	L	PCT	GB
Minnesota	95	67	.586	—
Chicago	87	75	.537	8
Texas	85	77	.525	10
Oakland	84	78	.519	11
Seattle	83	79	.512	12
Kansas City	82	80	.506	13
California	81	81	.500	14

Toronto, too, had a legacy of unfulfilled potential—it had dropped league championship series in 1985 and 1989, and had lost a heartbreaker of a title race to Detroit in 1987. Two franchises that (like Rodney Danger-field) got no respect were about to slug it out for the pennant.

The best-of-seven playoff series began in Toronto on October 8th and pitted Jack Morris against knuckleballer Tom Candiotti in the opener. Minnesota hitters were ready for Candiotti's tricks. In his book *Season of Dreams*, Twins manager Tom Kelly said, "We knew [Candiotti] started hitters with the knuckleball, then when he fell behind in the count, he threw breaking balls. If he went 3-0, then he mixed in a little cutter [moving fast-ball]. We had the right idea on what he was going to throw." Patience at the plate worked for Minnesota, and they took the first game, 5-4. Twenty-one-year-old fireballer Juan Guzman shut the Twins down the next day at the Metrodome, 5-2, but Minnesota came back and won the next three games in a row—by scores of 3-2, 9-3, and 8-5—to glide to the pennant.

When stopper Rick Aguilera induced the final out of Game 5—a Sandy Alomar line drive right to Twins left fielder Dan Gladden—the

Twins poured onto the field to celebrate. Tom Kelly, usually a reserved and unemotional manager, trotted out of the dugout and hugged each of his players. After ending at the bottom of the standings in 1990, the longshot Minnesota Twins had won the 1991 American League pennant—and they looked like they had hardly broken a sweat.

★ ★ ★

The Braves, by contrast, would have to fight for every inch of ground in their battle for the National League pennant. At the end of September, Tom Lasorda's Dodgers, a capable crew of established superstars, held a scant one-game lead over Atlanta.

National League West Standings: September 30, 1991

TEAM	W	L	PCT	GB
Los Angeles	90	66	.577	—
Atlanta	**89**	**67**	**.571**	**1**
San Diego	80	76	.513	10
Cincinnati	74	82	.474	16

On October 1st, Dodger outfielder Darryl Strawberry smashed his second homer in as many days to carry his team to victory over the San Diego Padres. The scrappy Braves were undaunted, and they rallied in the ninth inning behind a dramatic two-run blast by David Justice to notch a come-from-behind win over the Reds and remain just one game behind Los Angeles. Things were getting tight; only four games remained on Atlanta's schedule.

The next day, Strawberry hit yet another home run for the Dodgers, but it wasn't enough. The Padres enjoyed a six-run eighth inning off reliever Kevin Gross to break the game wide open and top Los Angeles, 9-4.

Over in Cincinnati, the Braves were poised to make their move. Starter Tom Glavine got all the support he needed in the first inning; the Braves pounded Cincinnati pitching for six runs at the game's outset. Glavine went eight innings, giving up three runs—only one earned—to notch his 20th victory of the year. Alejandro Pena finished the Reds off to earn his 14th save; the Braves won, 6-3. Meanwhile, in Los Angeles, the October 3rd headlines read, rather desperately, "Braves tie up Dodgers!"

National League West Standings: October 3, 1991				
TEAM	W	L	PCT	GB
Atlanta	**92**	**67**	**.579**	—
Los Angeles	92	67	.579	—
San Diego	81	78	.509	11
Cincinnati	74	85	.465	18

After both Los Angeles and Atlanta had a travel day, the Braves found themselves back home for a final three-game series against the last-place Houston Astros. That evening, young Steve Avery tossed $6\frac{2}{3}$ innings of no-hit ball to coast to a 5-2 win—his 18th on the year. After the game, Bobby Cox marveled, "Steve looked like a seasoned veteran out there."

The Dodgers played out their schedule in San Francisco and were handily topped by the Giants, 4-1, that same Friday evening. Atlanta was alone at the top of the standings with two games to go.

On Saturday, October 5th, John Smoltz hurled a complete game, 5-2 victory over the hapless Astros. At the All-Star break, Smoltz had been a pitiful 2-11, but after slightly adjusting his delivery, he found his form and wound up at 14-13. Thanks to his clutch performance, the Braves had clinched at least a tie for first place in the West.

The Dodgers-Giants game was not yet over; the entire Braves roster stood on the Fulton County Stadium turf, intently watching the Dodgers game on the Diamondvision scoreboard. Over 45,000 Atlanta fans watched with them. A Dodger loss would bring Atlanta its first division title in nine years. The fans chanted "Beat L.A." at a deafening volume while tomahawking maniacally. Finally, the last out was recorded in San Francisco; the Giants had shut out the Dodgers, 4-0. The city of Atlanta went berserk.

Afterwards, an emotional Tom Glavine confessed that the road to the title had not been easy: "To have had four years as miserable as they've been, as frustrating as they've been, has been tough." Charlie Leibrandt praised his newest teammates: "Terry Pendleton and Sid Bream. They were the glue to this team. They wouldn't let us roll over and play dead. They deserve all the credit in the world."

Atlanta lost their season finale; the Dodgers won theirs to finish the year just a game behind Atlanta. Close but no cigar: the new Miracle Braves had taken the division and were off to Pittsburgh for the playoffs.

"Facing [the Pirates in the playoffs] will be great," said a pumped-up Sid Bream. "I'm just hoping we can take four straight."

Final 1991 National League West Standings

TEAM	W	L	PCT	GB
Atlanta	94	68	.580	—
Los Angeles	93	69	.574	1
San Diego	84	78	.519	10
San Francisco	75	87	.463	19
Cincinnati	74	88	.457	20
Houston	65	97	.401	29

Taking four straight from the heavily favored Pirates would be a tall order. The Braves' grueling photo-finish pennant scramble had taken its toll; the team was more fatigued than Bobby Cox wanted to admit. The Pirates, on the other hand, had long ago clinched the National League East and ended their season a comfortable 14 games in front of second-place St. Louis. They had posted the best record in either league. They were well rested and hungry to head into the postseason.

The Braves' ace, Tom Glavine, faltered in Game 1 of the playoffs and the Pirates had the advantage, winning by a score of 5-1. Atlanta came back the next day and squeaked by, 1-0, on a masterful Steve Avery shutout. Two days later, the Braves went up two games to one in the series when they rocked John Smiley and the Pirates, 10-3. Game 4 was a nail-biter, but Pittsburgh prevailed, 4-3, in ten innings. The series was tied at two games apiece.

While Minnesota pitchers took batting practice and bunting drills in preparation for the fall classic, the Pirates and Braves were taking things to the limit. Pitching had now become the true name of the game for both clubs. Pittsburgh won Game 5 by a score of 1-0, but Atlanta bore down and took Game 6 by the same tight score. The National League pennant would be decided in the seventh game.

Atlanta starter John Smoltz, winner of Game 3, was on the mound against John Smiley, loser of Game 3. The big Atlanta righthander showed what he was made of as he shut out the Pirates by a score of 4-0 to capture the National League flag.

The pennant had landed in the city of Atlanta for the first time ever, and the city was relishing every minute of it. Like the Braves fans of 1914, Atlanta partisans could point to an utterly unpredictable league championship. Unlike the Boston faithful of seventy-seven seasons earlier, they could not claim that theirs was the only team in the World Series by means of a miracle.

★　★　★

The most unlikely World Series in baseball history opened in Minneapolis on Saturday, October 19, 1991.

In the opener, Jack Morris brought his career post-season record up to 6-1 when he went seven-plus innings en route to a 5-2 victory; Rick Aguilera came on in the ninth to save it. Minnesota won the first game in front of the home crowd.

The Twins went up two games to none the next evening with the help of home runs by Chili Davis and rookie Scott Leius. It marked the first rookie home run in a World Series game since Willie McGee's in 1982. Also aiding the Twins were some Metrodome ceiling-induced errors on the Braves part. Most of the Atlanta players had never set foot in the Metrodome, and they were horrified when they first caught sight of the shiny, light gray ceiling. In the end, Kevin Tapani won it, 3-2, for the Twins while Tom Glavine took the tough loss.

The Series moved to Fulton County Stadium, where Atlanta residents were still swooning over their team's pennant victory. Now the Twins had to play by National League rules: no designated hitters. Chili Davis was considered too much of a defensive liability to play in the field, but his bat would be sorely missed by the Twins.

Game 3 was a drama of epic proportions. The Braves let the Twins chip away at a 4-1 lead to tie the game in the eighth, and the deadlock held in the ninth. Both teams battled past midnight into the twelfth inning. In the bottom of the twelfth, with two outs and David Justice at second, Gary Lemke stroked a clutch single to left. It was not hit particularly deep, but Justice never let up and slid in under the throw for the winning run.

Atlanta went wild. And that means *all* of Atlanta. Commercial flights had been delayed (with no protests) so that passengers and crew could catch the end of the nail biter. In the sports-bar district of Buckhead, fans crowded into the narrow doorways of taverns. Broadcasts of the game were projected onto the sides of buildings for the public. When the Braves finally prevailed, a strange air of unreality hung over the city as the huge party disbanded.

Game 4 was no less exciting. With the score tied, 1-1, in the fifth inning, Braves outfielder Lonnie Smith was on second when Pendleton hit a towering blast to deep center. Kirby Puckett raced back, but clearly had no play. For reasons that still mystify Atlantans, Smith—representing the go-ahead run—held up at second. When the ball sailed past Puckett, Smith took off and tried to score, but it was too late. Puckett rifled a strike to the plate, Brian Harper nabbed it and braced himself for a collision with Smith. The runner came in hard, but Harper was able to hang onto the ball and Smith was out by a country mile. It wouldn't be his last running error of the Series.

Smith's mistake cost the Braves a run, but Atlanta came around to win the game in the bottom of the ninth on a sacrifice fly by pinch-hitter Jerry Willard. Shane Mack made a strong throw to try to catch the swift Mark Lemke. It was a close play at the plate, but Lemke evaded Harper's tag. The big catcher howled at umpire Terry Tata, but to no avail. The game was over. The Braves had tied up the Series by winning two games in a row—and in both games, the winning run had been scored on a close play at the plate to end the game. Atlanta fans were exhausted but ecstatic. It seemed as if no one in the city had gotten to work on time in months.

Game 5 was the only blowout of the Series. Atlanta hitters shellacked everything the Twins had to offer. They sprayed 17 hits for 14 runs and won their third game in a row, 14-5. Fulton County Stadium was filled with the deafening sounds of chants and drums. Atlanta fans were convinced that their team's momentum would be enough to carry them to at least one victory in the nasty Metrodome. Twins fans were, as usual, nervous.

Back at the Metrodome on October 26th, it was time for another nailbiter. The two clubs took a 2-2 game into the 11th inning. Kirby Puckett led off the bottom of the 11th against veteran Braves pitcher Charlie Leibrandt. Puckett smashed a 2-1 changeup over the wall in deep left-center. As Puckett sprinted around the bases pumping his fist in the air, radio announcer John Gordon screamed into his microphone, "The Twins are going to the seventh game!" Minnesota had tied up the Series, and they had done so in thrilling fashion.

The seventh and deciding game was played the next day. In the most important game of his managerial career, Tom Kelly started his workhorse, Jack Morris. John Smoltz went to the mound for the Braves. The two pitchers battled it out inning after inning, scattering hits and walks, but refusing to allow a run.

In the eighth inning of the scoreless ballgame, the Braves had a golden opportunity to take the lead. Lonnie Smith started off with a single to right. Terry Pendleton then stepped up and hit a screaming line drive towards the gap in left center. Smith was running with the pitch, but with his head down—he had no idea where the ball was. Twins second baseman Chuck Knoblauch, noticing Smith's confusion, pretended to field the ball and flip it to shortstop Greg Gagne to start a double play. Smith, faked out of his socks, stopped at second, looking for the ball. What seemed like an eternity (for Braves fans) passed before Smith realized the ball was still being tracked down in the outfield. He hustled over to third but had to stay there; he would surely have scored had he looked up or to the third base coach. Smith's second costly running error of the series would loom large over the winter.

Morris bore down and got Ron Gant to ground out. After intentionally walking David Justice, the Twins pulled off a flawless first-to-catcher-to-first double play. Unbelievably, Morris had gotten out of the jam unscathed.

The game remained scoreless into the tenth inning, becoming only the second Game 7 in World Series history to go to extra innings. When Kelly hinted that he was considering taking Morris out of the game, the feisty righthander growled that there was no game to rest up for the next day. He pitched the tenth. Nobody scored.

In the bottom of the tenth, Dan Gladden stroked a double to left center. Knoblauch laid down a perfect sacrifice bunt, sending Gladden to third. The world championship was 90 feet from home plate, with Puckett and Hrbek due up. Braves reliever Alejandro Pena intentionally walked both of the heavy hitters. Pinch-hitter Gene Larkin strode to the plate. The bases were full; all that was needed was a fly ball. Larkin delivered it.

The ball sailed over the pulled-in outfielders' heads. Gladden trotted home, stomped on the plate, and ended the game. Pandemonium swept through the Metrodome. Minnesota was for real; the curse was over

★ ★ ★

The Twins somehow managed to don freshly-printed World Championship T-shirts and caps; the team ran an impromptu victory lap around the field. Tom Kelly came out of the dugout and, in a gesture too rarely seen in baseball these days, shook hands with and congratulated members of the Atlanta Braves. (Before the first at-bat of the seventh game, the Braves' Lonnie Smith had reached down to shake hands with Twins catcher Brian Harper.)

After the game, Jack Morris was asked how many innings he could have pitched. He deadpanned, "Probably 112." Later, he summed up the historic contest in his own no-nonsense way, "It was flat-out a beautiful ballgame." And a beautiful series. Morris was named MVP.

"Words don't describe the respect I would like to give [Jack Morris]," said Braves outfielder David Justice after the game. "He's a battler. He never stops battling." Indeed, it was almost frightening to watch Jack Morris get better and better as the game went on. Had there been a Game 8, he would no doubt have lobbied to start it as well.

"I wish I could split it in half," said an exuberant Tom Kelly while holding the huge World Series trophy aloft. "I can't say who played better." All told, three of the seven games had gone to extra innings—a World Series record. Five games had been decided by just one run, with four of them ending on a final swing of the bat.

Certainly the 1912, 1947, and 1975 seasons should be remembered for their classic World Series play. But 1991 was a strange year, and when baseball commissioner Fay Vincent proclaimed the Twins-Braves epic the "greatest World Series ever," few could disagree.

Every classic World Series has its goat, and 1991 was no exception. Braves fans would be haunted by the memory of Lonnie Smith's eighth-inning baserunning blunder in the final game.

In his coverage of the Smith incident, *Boston Globe* sportswriter Steve Fainaru wrote: "This will be no solace to him in his old age, but the World Series needed Lonnie Smith to be standing there in the eighth inning

Sunday . . . Smith was the final piece to this perfect Series—he was the mystery that we can take with us into winter and all the winters to come. In a truly historic game, with no score and the nation riveted, the man simply stopped in his tracks. We'll probably never know exactly why."

★   ★   ★

Though they missed winning the 1991 World Series by the skin of their teeth, the Braves, as a franchise, remain unique. They are one of only a handful of teams to survive three geographical moves, and they are the only club that can lay claim to winning a pennant in each of its three locations: Boston in 1914 and 1948; Milwaukee in 1957 and 1958; and Atlanta in 1991 and 1992.

No matter what the future holds for the Braves, the franchise will now and always represent something special to diehard romantics. Twice in this century—a little less than a decade after it began and a little less than a decade before it ends—the Braves have done the impossible.

The Yankees may have had the dynasty, the Dodgers may have had the poetry, and the Red Sox may have had the heartache. But in two inconceivable seasons, three-quarters of a century and half a continent apart, the unlikely Braves demonstrated that they knew what made baseball, and America, tick: dreams.

CHAPTER TEN

HONORABLE MENTION

Space constraints kept these teams from receiving full examination in *Longshots*, but the following pages will provide a glimpse of what made their seasons special.

1919 CHICAGO WHITE SOX

Final 1919 American League Standings

TEAM	W	L	PCT	GB
Chicago	**88**	**52**	**.629**	—
Cleveland	84	55	.604	3½
New York	80	59	.576	7½
Detroit	80	60	.571	8
St. Louis	67	72	.482	20½
Boston	66	71	.482	20½
Washington	56	84	.400	32
Philadelphia	36	104	.257	52

Over the years, the infamous "Black Sox" gambling scandal has masked the fact that the 1919 Chicago White Sox were actually one of baseball's greatest longshot teams. In 1918, the team won just 57 of 114 games in a season abbreviated by World War I. The following year, they staved off Cleveland and the surging Yankees for the pennant. They had a pretty bleak pitching staff, with Ed Cicotte and Lefty Williams being the only real sparks. Of course, the rest is stomach-churning history: the Sox threw the World Series, allowing the Cincinnati Reds to win. As a result, eight Chi-town players were banned from baseball for life. But the fact remains that they took the A.L. flag fair and square with only a pair of reliable starting pitchers.

1926 NEW YORK YANKEES

Final 1926 American League Standings

TEAM	W	L	PCT	GB
New York	**91**	**63**	**.591**	—
Cleveland	88	66	.571	3
Philadelphia	83	67	.553	6
Washington	81	69	.540	8
Chicago	81	72	.529	9½
Detroit	79	75	.513	12
St. Louis	62	92	.403	29
Boston	46	107	.301	44½

The Bronx Bombers had won three straight A.L. titles from 1921-23. In 1925, however, they dropped to seventh place. Babe Ruth didn't play until June because of his celebrated "stomach abscess." The Ruth-less Yankees finished in seventh, 28½ games out of first place. Things were different in '26. Ruth came back and led them to a 91-63 season as well as the A.L. pennant. They lost the seventh and final game of the World Series by one run to the St. Louis Cardinals. Picked for third or fourth at the beginning of the season, this was virtually the same team that, in 1927, would be hailed as the greatest in baseball history.

1930 ST. LOUIS CARDINALS

Final 1930 National League Standings

TEAM	W	L	PCT	GB
St. Louis	**92**	**62**	**.597**	—
Chicago	90	64	.584	2
New York	87	67	.565	5
Brooklyn	86	68	.558	6
Pittsburgh	80	74	.519	12
Boston	70	84	.455	22
Cincinnati	59	95	.383	33
Philadelphia	52	102	.338	40

In 1929, the Cardinals had finished in fourth place, 20 games out of first. The next year, in the middle of August, they found themselves in fourth again, just one game over .500. Baseball followers had just written the club off when something snapped. Maybe the players realized that their uniforms weren't getting quite dirty enough. Whatever it was, they went on a tear, playing hard and rough, and winning 39 of their last 49 games to edge out the Cubs, Giants and Dodgers in one of baseball's most underrated pennant runs. With every one of their regulars hitting over .300, the Cardinals ended the year with a .314 team batting average.

1935 CHICAGO CUBS

Final 1935 National League Standings

TEAM	W	L	PCT	GB
Chicago	**100**	**54**	**.649**	—
St. Louis	96	58	.623	4
New York	91	62	.595	8½
Pittsburgh	86	67	.562	13½
Brooklyn	70	83	.458	29½
Cincinnati	68	85	.444	31½
Philadelphia	64	89	.418	35½
Boston	38	115	.248	61½

They spent most of the season in second or third place after finishing third the year before. On Labor Day of 1935, with Chicago still mired in third and seemingly out of contention, Cubs radio announcer Ronald "Dutch" Reagan proclaimed facetiously that if the Cubs wanted to win the pennant, they'd have to win all of their remaining games. Cubbie fans chuckled sadly. But the team proceeded to win 21 consecutive games—enough to clinch the pennant. They couldn't keep up the pace in the World Series, though; the Detroit Tigers took them in six games. Still, it had been a remarkable September in Chicago.

1942 ST. LOUIS CARDINALS

Final 1942 National League Standings

TEAM	W	L	PCT	GB
St. Louis	**106**	**48**	**.688**	—
Brooklyn	104	50	.675	2
New York	85	67	.559	20
Cincinnati	76	76	.500	29
Pittsburgh	66	81	.449	36½
Chicago	68	86	.442	38
Boston	59	89	.399	44
Philadelphia	42	109	.278	62½

Keeping pace with the surging Dodgers for most of the season, the Cards suddenly dropped to 10½ back in August, and things looked bleak. But Stan Musial and Enos Slaughter led the way in one of the great baseball comebacks. Even with the Dodgers winning ten of their last twelve contests, St. Louis lost only four games in the entire month of September to win the pennant. They then easily downed the New York Yankees to win the World Series.

1946 BOSTON RED SOX

Final 1946 American League Standings

TEAM	W	L	PCT	GB
Boston	**104**	**50**	**.675**	—
Detroit	92	62	.597	12
New York	87	67	.565	17
Washington	76	78	.494	28
Chicago	74	80	.481	30
Cleveland	68	86	.442	36
St. Louis	66	88	.429	38
Philadelphia	49	105	.318	55

No major league baseball team has ever improved as dramatically as the Red Sox did in '46. The team was 71-83 in 1945, which left them in seventh place in the American League. A year later they won 33 more games, the biggest improvement ever by a pennant-winner. Credit for the improvement, however, goes more to Douglas MacArthur and Dwight Eisenhower than to anyone in the Boston front office. Everyday players like Bobby Doerr, Johnny Pesky, Dom DiMaggio, and, of course, Ted Williams returned to the Sox lineup after stints in the military; Tex Hughson, Mickey Harris and Joe Dobson rejoined the pitching rotation. With the returning war veterans, the Red Sox bore little resemblance to the second-rate Boston squad of 1945. While Boston may have been a longshot at the start of the season, their odds improved dramatically once Williams and friends came back from the war.

1954 NEW YORK GIANTS

Final 1954 National League Standings

TEAM	W	L	PCT	GB
New York	**97**	**57**	**.630**	—
Brooklyn	92	62	.597	5
Milwaukee	89	65	.578	8
Philadelphia	75	79	.487	22
Cincinnati	74	80	.481	23
St. Louis	72	82	.468	25
Chicago	64	90	.416	33
Pittsburgh	53	101	.344	44

They jumped from a fifth-place 70-84 finish in '53 to a 97-57 pennant-winning year in '54. They welcomed Willie Mays (.345, 41 homers) back from a spell in the Army. They made a trade of genius proportions by sending the hero of '51, Bobby Thomson (broken ankle/generally washed up) to Milwaukee for pitcher Johnny Antonelli (21-7, 2.29 ERA). Most impressively, however, they swept the Cleveland Indians, winners of 111 regular season games, in the World Series.

1959 LOS ANGELES DODGERS

Final 1959 National League Standings

TEAM	W	L	PCT	GB
Los Angeles	**88**	**68**	**.564**	—
Milwaukee	86	70	.551	2
San Francisco	83	71	.539	4
Pittsburgh	78	76	.506	9
Chicago	74	80	.481	13
Cincinnati	74	80	.481	13
St. Louis	71	83	.461	16
Philadelphia	64	90	.416	23

Having finished in seventh place the previous year, the newly-relocated Dodgers came alive in '59. Seasoned veterans Gil Hodges, Duke Snider and Jim Gilliam worked beautifully alongside youngsters Don Drysdale, Sandy Koufax, and John Roseboro. L.A.'s rollercoaster season ended in a first-place tie with the defending champion Milwaukee Braves. L.A. swept Milwaukee in a three-game playoff series and beat the Go-Go White Sox four games to two in the World Series.

1961 CINCINNATI REDS

Final 1961 National League Standings

TEAM	W	L	PCT	GB
Cincinnati	**93**	**61**	**.604**	—
Los Angeles	89	65	.578	4
San Francisco	85	69	.552	8
Milwaukee	83	71	.539	10
St. Louis	80	74	.519	13
Pittsburgh	75	79	.487	18
Chicago	64	90	.416	29
Philadelphia	47	107	.305	46

In 1960, the Pittsburgh Pirates were the talk of baseball. They had taken the pennant and upset the mighty Yankees in the World Series. That same year, the Cincinnati Reds were also-rans, finishing 28 games out of first with a .435 winning percentage. But what a difference a year can make. Joey Jay came over from the Braves and won 21 games for the '61 Reds. Jim O'Toole came into his own, winning 19 games. Youngster Vada Pinson tore the cover off the ball, batting .343. The team coasted to the pennant against all odds. Unfortunately for Cincinnati, the '61 Yankees—featuring a couple of guys named Roger and Mickey—ranked among history's greatest teams, and the Reds lost the World Series in five games.

1961 LOS ANGELES ANGELS

Final 1961 American League Standings

TEAM	W	L	PCT	GB
New York	109	53	.673	—
Detroit	101	61	.623	8
Baltimore	95	67	.586	14
Chicago	86	76	.531	23
Cleveland	78	83	.484	30½
Boston	76	87	.469	33
Minnesota	70	90	.438	38
Los Angeles	**70**	**91**	**.435**	**38½**
Kansas City	61	100	.379	47½
Washington	61	100	.379	47½

Okay, okay, so the Angels didn't win the pennant in '61. In fact, they didn't even contend. But they managed to set a little-known record that deserves mention here: the fledgling Angels won 70 games that year, the most ever by a first year expansion team. When a team finishes its premier season at a .435 clip, it has truly earned longshot status.

1964 ST. LOUIS CARDINALS

Final 1964 National League Standings

TEAM	W	L	PCT	GB
St. Louis	**93**	**69**	**.574**	—
Cincinnati	92	70	.568	1
Philadelphia	92	70	.568	1
San Francisco	90	72	.556	3
Milwaukee	88	74	.543	5
Los Angeles	80	82	.494	13
Pittsburgh	80	82	.494	13
Chicago	76	86	.469	17
Houston	66	96	.407	27
New York	53	109	.327	40

With four teams in serious contention for the pennant, the Cards of '64 put together a hot streak that coincided with the front-running Phillies' legendary collapse and clinched the pennant on the final day of the season. They had been in sixth place as late as August. Bear in mind, also, that this was a team that boasted the immortal Bob Uecker.

1973 NEW YORK METS

Final 1973 National League East Standings				
TEAM	W	L	PCT	GB
New York	**82**	**79**	**.509**	—
St. Louis	81	81	.500	1½
Pittsburgh	80	82	.494	2½
Montreal	79	83	.488	3½
Chicago	77	84	.478	5
Philadelphia	71	91	.438	11½

The Mets had been in last place as late as August 26th. In just a month and a half, the post-miracle Mets beat out the Cardinals, Pirates, Expos, and Cubs in the closest five-team pennant race in baseball history. If there is any tarnish on New York's divisional title victory, it may be that they set the dubious record of having the lowest winning percentage (just .509) by a first-place finisher. No other N.L. East team had a winning record. On the other hand, the Mets managed to shut down the Big Red Machine in the playoffs and to stretch the World Series to seven games against the powerful Oakland A's. Willie Mays bid adieu to baseball wearing a Mets uniform in this series. Somehow it was a fitting farewell to the "kid" who, 22 years earlier, had seen the New York Giants pull off the Miracle at Coogan's Bluff in his rookie season.

(The '51 Giants lost their Series, too.)

1980 PHILADELPHIA PHILLIES

Final 1980 National League East Standings

TEAM	W	L	PCT	GB
Philadelphia	**91**	**71**	**.562**	—
Montreal	90	72	.556	1
Pittsburgh	83	79	.512	8
St. Louis	74	88	.457	17
New York	67	95	.414	24
Chicago	64	92	.395	27

Throughout the final two months of the 1980 season, the Phils battled their fans, the media, and the pesky Montreal Expos. They won the N.L. East title on the last day of the season in a dramatic showdown with Montreal. In the end, rookie manager Dallas Green led his troops to a World Series triumph over the heavily favored Kansas City Royals. A million fans crowded the streets for the team's tickertape parade.

1984 CHICAGO CUBS

Final 1984 National League East Standings

TEAM	W	L	PCT	GB
Chicago	**96**	**65**	**.596**	—
New York	90	72	.556	6½
St. Louis	84	78	.519	12½
Philadelphia	81	81	.500	15½
Montreal	78	83	.484	18
Pittsburgh	75	87	.463	21½

In '83, the hapless Cubbies finished just three games above the last place Mets. But it was a rebuilding year, and by June of 1984, the reconstruction process was complete. Chicago acquired ace hurler Rick Sutcliffe (16-1) and breezed to the division title. Unfortunately, they broke their fans' hearts by losing the N.L. playoffs to the Padres after leading that series two games to none.

1985 KANSAS CITY ROYALS

Final 1985 American League West Standings

TEAM	W	L	PCT	GB
Kansas City	**91**	**71**	**.562**	**—**
California	90	72	.556	1
Chicago	85	77	.525	6
Minnesota	77	85	.475	14
Oakland	77	85	.475	14
Seattle	74	88	.457	17
Texas	62	99	.385	28½

Dick Howser managed the Royals to the team's sixth division title in eleven years. To be sure, George Brett, Steve Balboni, and Bret Saberhagen led a powerful squad. What made the '85 Royals a longshot is the way the team kept coming back from seemingly insurmountable setbacks in the latter part of the season. They clinched the division late, having spent most of the campaign in second place behind the Angels. They then recovered from a three-games-to-one deficit in the A.L. playoffs to take the pennant from Toronto. (Lucky for them, it was the first year the flag was decided by a best-of-seven playoff rather than a best-of-five.) To top it all off, the team pulled off an incredible comeback in the World Series against the St. Louis Cardinals, overcoming *another* three-games-to-one situation—with a little help from umpire Don Denkinger, who made a bad call in the Royals' favor in Game 6.

1987 MINNESOTA TWINS

Final 1987 American League West Standings

TEAM	W	L	PCT	GB
Minnesota	**85**	**77**	**.525**	—
Kansas City	83	79	.512	2
Oakland	81	81	.500	4
Seattle	78	84	.481	7
Chicago	77	85	.475	8
Texas	75	87	.463	10
California	74	87	.463	10

In '86 the Twins finished a dismal 21 games behind first-place California. Even the most optimistic Minnesota fans viewed the next year as a transitional "rebuilding" (or, perhaps more accurately, "building") period. But Kirby Puckett and company shook off the dead wood and forged a winning year in '87. After the Twins clinched the A.L. West division, fans had to bristle when they dropped their final five regular season games. But the faithful were rewarded. In the playoffs, the Twins breezed by the Tigers, and then staged a remarkable come-from-behind World Series victory, overcoming the Cardinals four games to three. It marked the first world championship for the Minnesota franchise.

"Just good enough, gentlemen," author Bill James would write, "just barely good enough."

1988 LOS ANGELES DODGERS

Final 1988 National League West Standings

TEAM	W	L	PCT	GB
Los Angeles	**94**	**67**	**.584**	—
Cincinnati	87	74	.540	7
San Diego	84	78	.516	11
San Francisco	83	79	.512	11½
Houston	82	80	.506	12½
Atlanta	54	106	.338	39½

Tommy Lasorda's crew posted two consecutive 73-89 seasons before easily clinching the 1988 N.L. West title, overcoming a strong Mets squad in the playoffs, and overcoming the heavily favored A's in the World Series, four games to one. L.A. pitching boasted a 2.03 ERA in the Series and held Oakland's big bats to a collective .177 whimper. The Dodgers' fantastic journey was epitomized by battle-worn Kirk Gibson's pinch-homer off Dennis Eckersley in Game 1.

1989 BALTIMORE ORIOLES

Final 1989 American League East Standings

TEAM	W	L	PCT	GB
Toronto	89	73	.549	—
Baltimore	**87**	**75**	**.537**	**2**
Boston	83	79	.512	6
Milwaukee	81	81	.500	8
New York	74	87	.460	14½
Cleveland	73	89	.451	16
Detroit	59	103	.364	30

Picked for last—they finished 34½ games back with a .335 winning percentage in 1988—the O's *almost* won the division in 1989. This was essentially the same team that set an agonizing record by losing its first 21 games just a year before. Manager Frank Robinson did an excellent job with the new faces while Cal Ripken and the other vets came out of the woodwork to finish the year in second place—just two games behind the division-winning Blue Jays.

SPORTSWRITERS' CREDITS

The following sports journalists participated in the informal survey that was conducted to select baseball's longshot teams. Without their help, this book wouldn't have happened. Again, I thank each one of them:

Kent Baker, *Baltimore Sun*
Bill Ballou, *Worcester Telegram & Gazette*
Rod Beaton, *USA Today*
Harland Beery, retired (formerly with the *Bremerton Sun*)
Furman Bisher, *Atlanta Journal*
Hal Bock, Associated Press
Steve Booher, *St. Joseph News-Press*
Bob Broeg, *St. Louis Post-Dispatch*
Bob Brookover, *Courier-Post*
Pete Cava, International Sports Associates
Dave Chase, *Baseball America*
Randy Covitz, *Kansas City Star*
Jerry Crasnick, *Cincinnati Post*
Tom Cushman, *San Diego Union-Tribune*
Rick Davis, *San Diego Tribune*
Tony DeMarco, *Fort Worth Star-Telegram*
Alan Eskew, Topeka Capital-Journal
Ray Finocchiaro, *Wilmington News-Journal*

Stan Hochman, *Philadelphia Daily News*
Dick Klayman, *New York Post*
Moss Klein, *Star-Ledger*
Jack Lang, SportsTicker
Mark Langill, *Pasadena Star-News*
Jack McCaffery, *Delaware County Daily Times*
Joe Minster, freelance writer
Terence Moore, *Atlanta Journal-Constitution*
Larry O'Rourke, *North Jersey Herald & News*
John Perrotto, *Beaver County Times*
Dan Shaughnessy, *Boston Globe*
Samuel J. Skinner Jr., Skinner's International News Services
Juan Vene, *El Diario*
Tom Verducci, *Newsday*
Gordon Verrell, *Long Beach Press-Telegram*

BIBLIOGRAPHY

Charles C. Alexander, *John McGraw.*
    The Viking Press, New York, 1988.
Baseball Digest. Magazine articles, 1991.
The Boston Globe. Newspaper articles, 1914-1992.
Jimmy Breslin, *Can't Anybody Here Play This Game?*
    The Viking Press, New York, 1963.
Stanley Cohen, *A Magic Summer.*
    Harcourt Brace Jovanovich, New York, 1988.
Ken Coleman and Dan Valenti, *The Impossible Dream Remembered: The
    1967 Red Sox.*
    Stephen Greene Press, Lexington, Massachusetts, 1987.
Tony Conigliaro and Jack Zanger, *Seeing it Through.*
    The Macmillan Company, New York, 1970.
John Warner Davenport, *Baseball's Pennant Races: A Graphic View.*
    First Impressions, Madison, WI, 1981.
Paul Dickson, *Baseball's Greatest Quotations.*
    Harper Collins, New York, 1991.
Leo Durocher, *Nice Guys Finish Last.*
    Simon & Schuster, New York, 1975.
Joseph Durso, *Amazing.*
    Houghton Mifflin Company, Boston, 1970.
Michael Gershman, *The 1989 Baseball Card Engagement Book.*
    Houghton Mifflin, Boston, 1988.
David Halberstam, *Summer of '49.*
    William Morrow, New York, 1989.

Donald Honig, *A Donald Honig Reader.*
Fireside Books, New York, 1988.
Jim Hunter and Armen Keteyian, *Catfish.*
McGraw Hill, New York, 1988.
Roger Kahn, *The Boys of Summer.*
Signet Books, New York, 1973.
Tom Kelly and Ted Robinson, *Season of Dreams.*
Voyageur Press, Stillwater, Minnesota, 1992.
Bill Madden and Moss Klein, *Damned Yankees.*
Warner Books, New York, 1990.
David S. Neft and Richard M. Cohen, *The World Series.*
St. Martin's Press, New York, 1990.
The New York Times. Newspaper articles, 1914-1991.
Marc Okkonen, *Baseball Uniforms of the 20th Century.*
Sterling Publishing, New York, 1991.
Daniel Okrent and Harris Lewine, eds., *The Ultimate Baseball Book.*
Houghton Mifflin, Boston, 1988.
Daniel Okrent and Steve Wulf, *Baseball Anecdotes.*
Oxford University Press, New York, 1989.
Dan Riley, ed., *The Red Sox Reader*, Revised Edition.
Houghton Mifflin, Boston, 1991.
Lawrence S. Ritter, *The Glory of Their Times.*
William Morrow, New York, 1966.
Lawrence S. Ritter and Donald Honig, *The Image of Their Greatness.*
Crown Publishers, New York, 1979.
George Robinson and Charles Salzberg, *On a Clear Day They Could See Seventh Place.*
Dell Publishing, New York, 1991.
Ray Robinson, *The Home Run Heard 'Round the World.*
Harper Collins, New York, 1991.
Mike Shatzkin and Jim Charlton, *The Ballplayers.*
Arbor House-William Morrow, New York, 1990.
Dan Shaughnessy, *The Curse of the Bambino.*
Penguin Books, New York, 1991.
Seymour Siwoff et al, *The 1991 Elias Baseball Analyst*
Fireside Books, New York, 1991.
Sports Illustrated. Magazine articles, 1985-1992.

Rick Talley, *The Cubs of '69.*
    Contemporary Books, Chicago, 1989.
John Thorn, ed., *The Armchair Book of Baseball II.*
    Charles Scribner's Sons, New York, 1987.
John Thorn and Pete Palmer, eds., *Total Baseball*
    Warner Books, New York, 1989
The Valley Advocate, Amherst, Massachusetts. Newspaper articles, 1978.
George Vecsey, *Joy in Mudville.*
    The McCall Publishing Company, New York, 1970.
Dick Williams, *No More Mr. Nice Guy*
    New York, 1990.
Carl Yastrzemski and Gerald Eskenazi, *Yaz: Baseball, the Wall, and Me.*
    Doubleday, New York, 1990.

INDEX